50 p

A S

CH00880745

Word 97

L. Steven

Prentice Hall Europe

London New York Toronto Sydney Tokyo Singapore Madrid
Mexico City Munich Paris

First published in 1997 as Word 97 – Se Former en 1 Jour by
Simon & Schuster Macmillan (France)
This edition published 1999 by
Prentice Hall Europe
Campus 400, Maylands Avenue
Hemel Hempstead
Hertfordshire, HP2 7EZ

A division of
Simon & Schuster International Group

Translated by Berlitz Translation Services UK, Baldock, Hertfordshire

Printed and bound in Great Britain by
Redwood Books, Trowbridge, Wiltshire

Library of Congress Cataloging-in-Publication Data

Available from the publisher

British Library Cataloguing in Publication Data

A catalogue record for this book is available from the British Library
ISBN 0-13-012197-5

1 2 3 4 5 03 02 01 00 99

Table of Contents

Hour 4

Introduction

WORD 97: COMMUNICATION AND SIMPLIFICATION

The main improvements made to the best-known word-processing program running in Windows 95 have made Word 97 a better communication tool. They simplify and improve the task of formatting.

SIMPLIFIED FORMATTING

Automatic formatting is one of the undoubted advances of this new version of the word-processing program. Headings, bulleted lists and numbered lists are applied automatically. A format is adapted to each type of document, regardless of whether it is a letter, an e-mail or a general document.

Real-time grammatical corrections

Spelling and grammatical correction while the text is being input is one of the major improvements offered by Word 97. The AutoCorrect function automatically corrects the majority of current typing errors, spelling errors and grammatical errors. Without prompting, it inserts text, graphics and symbols.

3D effects

One of the significant advances from Word 7 to Word 8, otherwise known as Word 97, is the facility for accessing 3D effects from the WordArt Toolbar. Documents are displayed in a far more attractive way. It has attained a degree of finish at least as good as that created by specialist printing and reprographic companies.

Automated contents list

A new and highly original function is the ability to generate an automated contents list at any time. The outline of the document appears to the right of the screen. The key phrases of the text and the significant words or groups of words appear at the left of the screen.

Straightforward tables

Compiling tables from a word-processing program is no longer a problem. They can be created easily and immediately, to an exceptionally high standard. Users who tended to stumble at this obstacle when working with earlier versions of the program should notice an improvement.

Using the Internet to communicate

Last, but by no means least, the most spectacular advance of this version over its predecessors is undoubtedly the link created between word-processing and the Internet. To gain access to the network of networks, all that's required is to click on the Internet Toolbar and enter the world of communication and information exchange. Word 97 is capable of creating HTML pages and generating hypertext links. The addresses (URLs) which designate the locations of web sites are activated immediately and the user can access them with a double-click. This word-processing program allows network users to share documents – an improvement which promotes group working and which may be used to encourage initiative.

To sum up, Word 97 is even more integrated into Office 97 than before and its macro language is Visual Basic Application 5.0. Macros can now be shared.

Throughout this document you will find notes, which you are at liberty to read or disregard. Each type of note is identified by an icon to help you locate it without difficulty:

These notes provide additional information about the subject concerned.

These notes indicate a variety of shortcuts: keyboard shortcuts, 'Wizard' options, techniques reserved for experts, etc.

These notes warn you of the risks associated with a particular action and, where necessary, show you how to avoid any pitfalls.

Hour 1

Learning about the software

THE CONTENTS FOR THIS HOUR

- Installing Word 97
- Starting Word 97
- Configuring Word 97
- Getting to know the Assistants
- Learning about the screen
- Using a dialog box

INSTALLING WORD 97

Word-processing is a valuable tool which is designed to assist you with the design and production of your documents. It is effective in both form and content. Word 97 is one of the most powerful software programs available on the market. It provides assistance to editorial professionals as well as to novices. It is easy to use and can be learned relatively quickly. In one day! Provided, of course, that you are prepared to follow our advice step by step.

Hardware requirements

To install and use Word 97 you must have:

- A PC with a 486 or Pentium processor
- Windows 95 (or a later version) or Windows NT
- At least 8 Mb of RAM (16 Mb for Windows NT)
- A hard disk with a minimum of 20 Mb disk space available for basic installation, 46 Mb for typical installation or 60 Mb for full installation
- A CD-ROM drive
- A Windows-compatible monitor
- A Microsoft-compatible mouse

Unlike ROM, which only permits read access, it is possible to read and write to RAM

Installing Word 97

To install Word 97, proceed as follows:

1. Switch on your computer and start up Windows.
2. Insert the Word 97 CD into your CD-ROM drive.
3. Select the Installation button.

4. Then follow the instructions as they appear in succession in the various dialog boxes of the installation program.

STARTING WORD 97

With your computer running, the first step is to start the application. To do this, click on the Start icon on the Taskbar at the base of the screen.

Figure 1.1: Click on the Start icon on the Taskbar

The Programs option displays the sub-menus, including Word 97.

If you use Word very frequently, add a shortcut to your Desktop. This will allow you to start Word without using the Start menu. To place a shortcut on the Desktop, select Winword.exe (C:\msoffice) in Windows Explorer and drag-and-drop onto the Desktop.

One you have started the word-processing program, a blank document will appear. The vertical insertion point indicates where your text will start. However, before you start entering the text, you will have to adjust your word-processing program to ensure that it executes your commands point by point. This is known as configuring Word 97.

Configuring Word 97

Configuring your word-processing program involves adapting it to
your own editorial requirements. These may include, for example,
the choice and size of a font.

Fonts

The term 'font' is used to define a set of characters belonging to the
same typestyle. To select the font Book Antiqua:

1. Open the Format menu

2. Select the Font menu

3. In the Font field, scroll through the list

4. Click on Book Antiqua

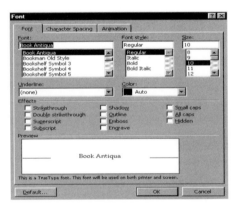

*Figure 1.2: Select the font Book Antiqua in the Font
dialog box with the Style and Effects tab*

Then select the font size. You can do this in two ways:

- By moving directly to the numerical field situated to the right of the field indicating the name of the font on the Formatting Toolbar of your word-processing program. With the pointer positioned on the numerical field, click on the downward-pointing black triangle to scroll through the menu. Then select the appropriate font size, for example 12.

- By opening the Format menu and selecting the Font command. Word 97 offers you a selection of some one hundred fonts and you can specify the size and the style in each case. It is possible to add other fonts which are commercially available on CD-ROM or on software programs.

You can view the fonts in greater detail in Chapter 3.

 Word 97 automatically installs fonts in a Windows directory called Fonts. The access path to this file is C:\Windows\Fonts. The majority of these are TrueType fonts. They are identified by the abbreviation TT. These fonts offer the advantage of providing you with a wide range of sizes and styles.

This command also allows you to set parameters such as fonts, character spacing and animations.

- On the Character Spacing tab you will find options relating to the spacing of the letters within a word, their position in relation to the line (above or below) and their scale.

- On the Animation tab you will find the options which are capable of creating an animation around the letters.

The Las Vegas animation, for example, surrounds each word with stars and flashing dots.

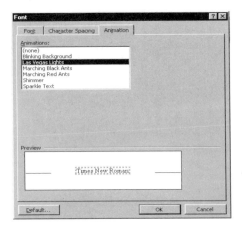

Figure 1.3: Select the Las Vegas animation in the Font dialog box, Animation tab

If you wish to make other adjustments before you start to compile your first document, the easiest way is to scroll through the Tools menu and select the Options command, which offers a wide choice of parameters relating to spelling and grammar, printing, views and editing. For example, you can specify that spelling and grammar be checked as you type.

Read through the options available in this dialog box; the majority of their names are self-explanatory. We will be dealing with the most important options throughout this document.

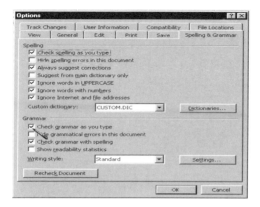

Figure 1.4: The "Check spelling as you type" and "Check grammar as you type" options

GETTING TO KNOW THE ASSISTANTS

Word 97 places nine Office Assistants at your disposal, to guide you through your word-processing journey. The Office Assistant is an interactive program.

Figure 1.5: The nine Word 97 Office Assistants

Each of these Assistants will respond at any time to any questions you have regarding specific tasks. To enlist their aid, click on the speech bubble, containing a question mark, in the upper right corner of your screen.

The Word Office Assistants are as follows:

Clippit	General guide
The Dot	Guide to the electronic frontier
The Genius (Einstein, of course!)	Guide to electronic space
Hoverbot	Getting more out of Office
Office Logo	Help with Office
Mother Nature	Help on any aspect of the program
Power Pup	Dynamic help with Office
Scribble, the origami cat	Guide to Office
Will (Shakespeare, that is!)	Guide to computers

In the dialog box that appears, indicate what you want to do. Once you have clearly phrased your question, you will have a choice of four selections:

- Search: initiate a search for a topic, a word or an idea you wish to have explained.

- Tips: the Office Assistant gives you a tip, in two or three lines, in response to the question you have raised.

- Options: allows you to set the selection of tips and options from the Office Assistant.

- Close: this option closes the dialog box.

If you enter the name of the Office Assistant and click on the Search/Clippit button, he will ask you if you want help with or without the Office Assistant or if you wish to choose a different one. If you wish, you can hide the Office Assistant, change his size, etc.

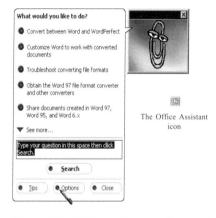

The Office Assistant icon

Figure 1.6: Click on the question mark icon to reveal the Office Assistant

If you click on Options, the Gallery and Options tabs appear on the screen.

The Office Assistant dialog box on the Options tab displays a series of boxes to be ticked, including:

- Respond to F1 key
- Help with wizards
- Make sounds
- Move when in the way
- Guess help topics
- Display alerts

Select the Office Assistant dialog box on the Gallery tab to find out more about Clippit, the impish paper clip, and the other eight Office Assistants.

However, to start with Clippit asks you what you would like to do and eagerly encourages you to proceed!

Click on the Next… command and you are introduced, in turn, to the other Office Assistants.

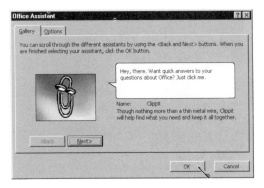

Figure 1.7: The Gallery tab allows you to scroll through the various Office Assistants

Clippit offers you a wealth of advice, like a wise and conscientious teacher.

If you have a specific question to ask him, indicate the key word(s) of the question in the text panel; for example, if you type 'Tabs', Clippit will display a selection of operations associated with tabulation. It is then up to you to select the one that corresponds to your question:

- Use tab stops
- Change the spacing between default tab stops, etc.

Figure 1.8: Clippit, the guide to solving problems

Let's say you want to insert tab stops. The Office Assistant displays a new list of operations, more precise each time:

- Set tab stops

- Clear or move tab stops

Figure 1.9: The Office Assistant accurately pinpoints your question

If you want to set tab stops, click on the white hand symbol on this command to obtain your answer.

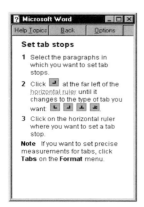

Figure 1.10: The Help panel displays the answer

The Assistant is used in all Office applications. Any changes you make to him in Word will also be applied in Office, Excel and PowerPoint.

LEARNING ABOUT THE SCREEN

You have started Word 97. You have configured its installation. You are now confronted by a default document. Before you start to use this page, familiarise yourself with the screen.

Pointer, scrolling menu, sub-menu, command, option, button, icon, dialog box, mouse button, Taskbar, Title bar, Menu bar, Toolbar, Status bar – which does what? What are they all for?

The Word 97 screen comprises five main elements:

- The Title bar
- The Menu bar

- The Toolbar

- The Status bar

- The document windows

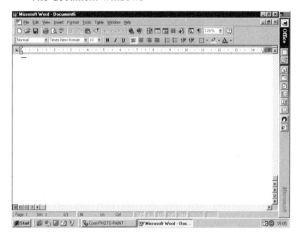

Figure 1.11: Learning about the Word 97 screen

The Status bar

The Status bar is the first bar you encounter when you start your installation, even before you select Word 97. It is situated at the base of the application window. It indicates valuable information about the various parameters displayed.

- The page displayed: the number of the page displayed is the first legible item to the left of the Status bar

- Section number: a section is defined by a skip between sections, with the number indicating the active section on the screen

- Number of the page displayed/total number of pages

- Position of the insertion point in relation to the upper edge of the page

- The line and column where the insertion point is located
- Operating modes:
    - REC: record active macros
    - REV: active revision marks
    - EXT: extension of the selection to the keyboard
    - OVR: overtype option
- Status of the spelling correction function at the end of the task

Figure 1.12: The Status bar

The Title bar

The Title bar is situated at the top of the screen.

The box for minimising and maximising the window is situated at the far right-hand end of this bar.

At the far left of the bar is an icon allowing you to close Word 97. The Title bar displays the name of the document.

W Microsoft Word - Document2

Figure 1.13: The Title bar

The Menu bar

The Menu bar is situated immediately below the Title bar. It comprises menus:

- The System menu
- File
- Edit

- View

- Insert

- Format

- Tools

- Table

- Window

- Help

Figure 1.14: The Menu bar

The toolbars

The toolbars are situated below the Menu bar.

Figure 1.15: Word 97 offers a range of toolbars

A number of toolbars can be displayed, according to your own preference. Word 97 allows you to customise your toolbars by adding two categories of tools:

- Those which already exist as standard and are accessible via the dialog box

- Those which you can create yourself with the aid of macros.

Macros are used to automate repetitive functions. You program them yourself (refer to Chapter 4).

To customise your toolbars, proceed as follows:

1. In the Tools menu, select the Customize option

2. Click on the Commands tab

3. Choose a category of commands

4. Scroll the commands to the selected category

5. Click on the ones you require

6. Drag them onto your Toolbar

Figure 1.16: The Customize dialog box and the Toolbars tab

Each icon is accompanied by a ScreenTip which explains its meaning. The ScreenTips can be deactivated. To do this:

1. Open the View menu

2. Select the Toolbars sub-menu

3. Choose the Customize option

4. Click on the Options tab of the Customize dialog box

5. Untick the Show ScreenTips box

Figure 1.17: Toolbar options

The ruler

The ruler is displayed in different ways, depending on the View mode and the position of the insertion point: in normal text, in a number of columns or in a table.

Figure 1.18: The ruler shows the tab stops

In Normal mode

The ruler shows the indent markers and tab stops in Page mode and the margin indicators are shown in grey. The type of tab currently in use is shown at the extreme left. Click on the tab stop to change the orientation:

- To the left

- To the centre

- To the right

- Decimal tab

These tab stops can be positioned with a single click. They can be inserted or removed by a drag-and-drop manoeuvre.

In Table mode

When the insertion point is in a table, the ruler shows the column divisions: drag-and-drop these to change the width of a column. The indent markers are indicated for the column you are currently working on.

The document window

Word 97 displays each document in a window which can be opened in standard or maximised form.

- To minimise the window: click on the Minimise window icon situated on the right-hand side of the Title bar.

- To restore the window to its original size: click on the Restore window icon situated on the right-hand side of the Title bar.

- To change from one window to another: you can open a number of document windows at the same time. To change from one to the other, press Ctrl+F6.

- To move a window: if a number of windows are displayed on the screen, it is sometimes necessary to move one of them. Using the mouse, drag the Title bar to the desired position.

- Sizing a window: using the mouse, move the pointer into one of the corners of the window. It then turns into a yellow bidirectional arrow. Drag it until you obtain the required size.

- To close the window: click on the Close window icon situated on the right-hand side of the Title bar. Closing a window releases space on your screen and in your memory.

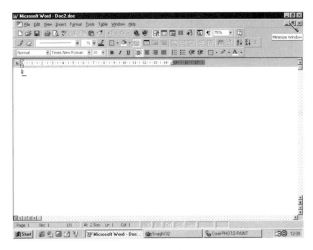

Figure 1.19: The Close window icon

The scroll bars

There are two scroll bars: a horizontal scroll bar at the base of the screen and a vertical scroll bar on the right of the screen. To move up or down through the text, drag the pointer as required.

To scroll the text from top to bottom, slide the pointer to the bottom or to the top.

To scroll the text from left to right, slide the pointer from left to right.

Figure 1.20: The pen is pointing to the vertical scroll bar

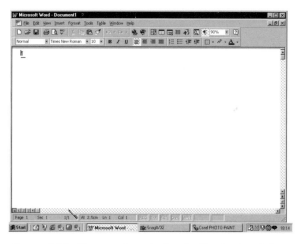

Figure 1.21: The pen is pointing to the horizontal scroll bar

▰▰▰ The pointers

The pointer is one of the most important working tools. It is the visual extension of the mouse on the screen. It can assume different forms according to the function in operation and position in which it is located.

As a general rule, the pointer is in the form of an arrow. A number of software programs allow you to create an animation around the pointers, such as pen pointers, galloping horses, dinosaurs, etc. These software programs are commercially available or they can be downloaded from the Internet.

The text pointer can be used to place the insertion point in the text by clicking on the chosen location. It takes the form of a capital I. The insertion point is placed in position by clicking on the chosen location. When the button is held down, the text is highlighted, with a black background and white letters.

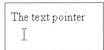

Figure 1.22: The text insertion point

To activate the drag-and-drop function, proceed as follows:

1. Select (highlight) the word you want to move

2. Hold down the mouse button

3. Drag the word. The pointer changes into a white arrow on a grey rectangle. This new pointer indicates that the selection, word or phrase will be moved.

Figure 1.23: The Drag-and-Drop pointer

The Magnifier pointer is displayed in Print Preview mode. It allows you to enlarge the view. When you are in Print Preview mode, select the magnifying glass icon and click on the area of text to be enlarged. This function allows you to view the page exactly as it will be printed.

Figure 1.24: The Magnifier pointer

The Resize pointer is used to move the margins in Print Preview mode.

It takes the form of a vertical double-headed arrow which changes to gold when it is placed on the ruler.

Figure 1.25: The Resize pointer

The Gridline pointer appears on the gridline. It turns into a vertical double-headed arrow when it is placed on the gridline.

Figure 1.26: The Gridline pointer

The Drawing pointer moves drawing elements in Drawing mode. It is in the form of a cross bearing four arrow heads. It can be used to select all the text attached to a heading level by clicking on the cross situated to the left of the heading in Drawing view.

Figure 1.27: The Drawing pointer

The Help pointer is in the form of a normal pointer with a gold question mark above it. You can call it up by clicking on the Question mark scrolling menu of your Title bar and selecting the option 'What's this?'.

Figure 1.28: The Help pointer

With this function selected, move your pointer to a keyword or to a part of the page you would like to have explained. An explanation then appears in a wide panel.

For example, if you move the Help pointer onto the scroll bar, you will obtain a sufficiently detailed response by clicking the left mouse button.

Don't worry! Over the next few hours you will have an opportunity to use all these terms in practice and by way of example!

USING A DIALOG BOX

The dialog boxes are designed to give you sufficiently complete – or even exhaustive – information on a given subject. They consist of a number of index cards which you can access by clicking on the tabs.

- Index cards: these are organised like files

- Radio knobs: these are used to select an option

- Tick boxes: these are activated by a single click with the left mouse button

- Text area: used to indicate a selection by entering text or numerical data

- Scrolling lists: these display a succession of options, which are selected by clicking on them.

- Counters: little boxes with arrows indicating up and down, for controlling a numerical count

- Command buttons: for confirming or cancelling a command

- Close box: the icon containing a multiplication symbol. It is situated in the upper right-hand corner of the dialog box. Click on it to close the active file.

Figure 1.29: The Break dialog box with its radio knobs and command buttons

Hour 2

Creating a document

THE CONTENTS FOR THIS HOUR

- Starting the easy way
- Writing a paragraph
- Moving through the text
- Amending the text
- Correcting the text
- Save or Save as

STARTING THE EASY WAY

When you start Word 97, the screen is ready for use. All you need to do is type the characters on the keyboard and they immediately appear on the screen. For this second hour of exercises, we will be using a text drawn from *Characters* by La Bruyère: *The Scatterbrain*. We will start by typing the title. But before that, there are a few points to note.

Insertion point and end-of-text marker

As you begin writing, you will be guided by two markers. The first is a vertical bar, measuring about half a centimetre, which blinks. This indicates where the next character will be inserted. For this reason, it is called the insertion point.

The second marker is a non-blinking horizontal bar, the same size as the blinking vertical bar. This underscore indicates the final limit of the text. As soon as you start to write, it moves to the right. If you skip a line, it moves downward.

|_

Figure 2.1: The insertion point, the start of your text

Inserting a title to the text

Type *The Scatterbrain*. As you type, the insertion point moves to the right.

Once you have typed *The Scatterbrain*, skip a few lines by pressing the Enter key several times.

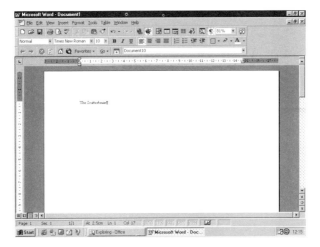

Figure 2.2: Movements of the insertion point

The horizontal end-of-text marker moves downward, as a number of line breaks have been introduced. 'Line break' is the accepted term for this action. All line breaks are generated by pressing the Enter key. They constitute a voluntary interruption of the text. They should only be used to separate blocks of text.

Until now, the insertion point and the end-of-text marker have been situated on the same line. To begin with, they were almost touching each other. Gradually, the insertion point moves away to the right while the end-of-text marker remains fixed at the left-hand side. Now that we have skipped four or five lines, they are close together once again.

WRITING A PARAGRAPH

To type the first paragraph, the insertion point must be moved up to the required position. To do this, lightly press the 'up' arrow

key a few times. The insertion point moves up. Stop it two lines below the title.

You can now type the complete paragraph, as shown in Figure 2.3. The appearance of your text is not important at the moment. You will be applying formatting at a later stage.

This is the quickest and most efficient way to proceed. For now, confine your efforts at continuous typing.

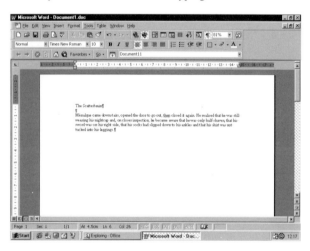

Figure 2.3: Continuous typing

▰▰▰ Automatic text wrap

As you type the text, you needn't concern yourself with line breaks. These are incorporated automatically. This flexibility is particularly useful when you begin to amend or insert text.

Choosing a view

Once you have typed the title and the first paragraph, you will have a coherent, temporary presentation. In Word 97, Normal view is the most suitable mode for continuous typing.

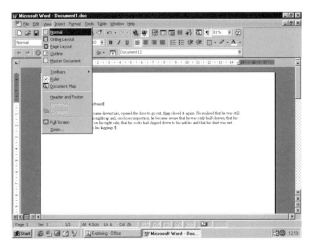

Figure 2.4: Normal view is the most suitable mode for continuous typing

If you want to change the way Word 97 displays the screen, click on View in the Menu bar. A scrolling list appears, containing a series of options and commands. Try selecting them in turn:

- Normal view: the default view for the majority of word-processing tasks (typing, amendments, formatting, etc.). Normal view is generally used for inputting text.

- Online Layout: this is most suitable for viewing and reading documents on-screen. In this mode, Word 97 also displays Windows Explorer, which you can use to easily access various parts of your document.

- Page Layout view: lets you view your document on the screen exactly as it will be printed or amended. This mode requires considerable system memory, which may slow down the scrolling speed of the document.

- Outline view: allows you to work on the structure of your document. You must use this mode to organise and develop the content of your files.

Choose the view which suits you best. Outline view is complex and is only used for initial work involving the creation of a simple document.

Selection buttons for the different types of view

The icons for selecting the different types of view are situated at the bottom of the screen when the display is in Normal view.

Figure 2.5: The icons for selecting the different types of view appear at the bottom of the screen

For the purposes of this exercise, select Page Layout view. It has the advantage of displaying two rulers, which act as reference points and allow you to decide on the position of the margins (as you will see further on).

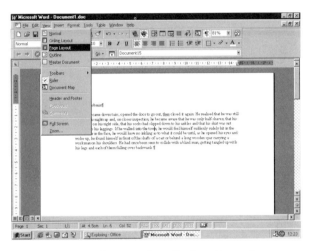

Figure 2.6: Page Layout view displays two rulers

The ruler allows you to position objects or to modify paragraph indents, margins or other spacing parameters.

MOVING THROUGH THE TEXT

When you type a text, it is often necessary to make improvements to the style or content. As far as amendments, deletions or additions are concerned, the first step is to position the cursor at the point you wish to edit.

There are two types of movement: lateral movement and scrolling (vertical movement).

Lateral movement

Lateral movement can be controlled with the mouse or from the keyboard. To move the insertion point using the mouse, simply click on the required area, which immediately becomes the active part of the text.

Keyboard shortcuts can also be used if you prefer not to use the mouse. Some people are totally averse to using the mouse!

To move laterally using the keyboard, use the following keys:

- Arrow left: to move one character to the left
- Arrow right: to move one character to the right
- Arrow up: to move up one line
- Arrow down: to move down one line
- Ctrl + arrow right: to move one word to the right
- Ctrl + arrow left: to move one word to the left

In the following, the numbers must be typed on the numeric keypad.

- Shift+7: move to the start of a line
- Shift+1: move to end of a line
- Shift+3: move one page down
- Shift+9: move one page up
- Ctrl+Alt + Page Down: move one page down
- Ctrl+Alt + Page Up: move one page up
- Ctrl+7: move to the start of the document
- Ctrl+1: move to the end of the document

Scrolling

Scrolling is controlled with the mouse. To scroll through a document, use the scrolling bars. There are two types: horizontal and vertical, more commonly referred to as elevators. To scroll the view vertically, just click the mouse on one of the two small black arrows at the top and bottom on the right-hand edge of the screen.

Figure 2.7: The vertical scroll bar

Scrolling can also be determined by 10 browse objects. To access these objects, click on the button situated at the base of the vertical elevator, between the two double black arrows. A small screen then appears, containing 12 boxes with the following ten options:

- Browse by Field

- Browse by Endnote

- Browse by Footnote

- Browse by Comment

- Browse by Section

- Browse by Page

- Browse by Edits

- Browse by Heading

- Browse by Graphic

- Browse by Table

Figure 2.8: The Select browse object button

Once you have selected your option – browse by Graphic, for example – click on the round button with the aid of the mouse. Your text will scroll, graphic by graphic.

Another highly practical function is the indicator panel which identifies the pages as you scroll through the document.

Let's assume that the document is ten pages long and you want to make an amendment to page 7: all you have to do is drag the elevator bar with the mouse in order to locate the exact page number.

Figure 2.9: The information panel indicates the page number

EDITING THE TEXT

The Clipboard

Word 97 uses the Clipboard tool. This can be used to temporarily store parts of documents or images and then copy them or paste them into another part of the document or into a different application.

Cutting and pasting a word

There are two ways of moving text or a word:

- The first is common to all applications running in Windows: this is the familiar Cut/Paste and Copy/Paste procedure used in conjunction with the Clipboard.

- The second is the Drag/Drop function.

Cutting and pasting a word is equivalent to placing it in the Clipboard before pasting it into a different position in the text. This operation involves cutting out the selected area using the key combination Ctrl+X. The same result is obtained by clicking on the Cut command in the Edit menu. The cut out area disappears: it has been transferred to the Clipboard.

1. Select the word. To do this with the mouse, place the pointer at either end of the word. Hold down the left mouse button as you move the pointer to the other end of the word. The word is then displayed in reverse video (highlighted).

2. Open the Edit menu

3. Click on the Cut command. The word then disappears from the screen.

4. Using the mouse, define the insertion point.

5. Open the Edit menu.

6. Click on the Paste command. The word is inserted at your chosen point in the text.

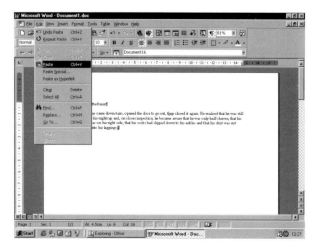

Figure 2.10: The Paste command in the Edit menu

It is also possible to use the keyboard shortcut Shift+Insert. The word is pasted into its new position. The text to the right of the insertion is automatically moved to accommodate the word. The line breaks are rearranged by Word 97. The text flows freely as far as the new location.

Copying and pasting a word

To copy a word, sentence, paragraph or text, proceed as follows:

1. Select the area in question.

2. Open the Edit menu.

3. Select the Copy function. The word or the text is moved to the Clipboard.

4. Next, place the insertion point in the required position.

5. Click on Paste.

▬▬ Dragging and dropping a word

In the following example, we have deliberately moved a word so that we can then replace it using the drag-and-drop method.

1. Using the mouse, select the part of the phrase reading 'Ménalque'.

2. Then position the mouse pointer on the lower edge of the selected passage. Click as soon as the pointer assumes the form of an inclined arrow, with the head pointing upward and to the left. The selected area is then captured by the mouse.

3. Drag your selection to the new location, at the end of the first sentence.

During the operation, the pointer is in the form of a small rectangle below the arrow. Yellow with a black border, it then turns white.

4. At the new location, when you release the mouse button, the text is inserted and everything returns to normal.

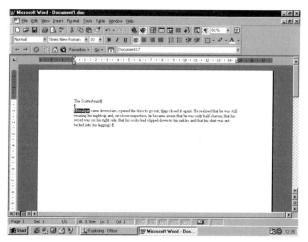

Figure 2.11: The Drag-and-Drop method

Word 97

Undoing and redoing a command

When making amendments to a text, you often need to proceed by
trial and error and you may want to undo an operation in order to
revert to the previous situation. For example, you may have placed
a word in a position which is not ideal. To cancel this operation, all
you need to do is select the Undo Typing icon.

Figure 2.12: The Undo Typing/Redo Typing icon

Word 97 has over 1,000 deletion levels. If you change your mind
again, you can also revert to the situation prior to the cancellation.
For this reason, it becomes less and less likely that you will make a
mistake.

Ctrl+Z to undo

Another way of cancelling an operation is to use the Ctrl (Control)
key, holding it down while you press the Z key. The Ctrl+Z key
sequence has the effect of cancelling the previous operation.

42

The first time you press Ctrl+Z, the amendment you have just made disappears.

▬▬▬ Ctrl+Y to redo

If you now press the Ctrl and Y keys simultaneously, the amendment disappears. If you press Ctrl+Y again, the amendment reappears. Cancelling and repetition are performed in an intelligent manner. Word 97 takes account of logic blocks. It does not work character by character.

CORRECTING THE TEXT

To select the spelling and grammar checkers when you have finished typing a text, perform the following operations:

1. Open the Tools menu.

2. Click on the Spelling and Grammar command or, to save time, click on the ABC icon. This is normally located between the magnifier icon and the icon representing a bold character.

Spelling correction is relatively straightforward. All you need to do is allow yourself to be guided by the suggestions displayed. You can either accept or disregard a suggestion or add unknown words to the dictionary. From then on, these will be recognised in the same way as those already stored in the dictionary.

In the text submitted for checking by the Spelling and Grammar Checkers, Word may highlight an uncommon word which does not appear in its dictionary or a proper name, such as, in our example, Ménalque.

You initial reaction should be to add the uncommon word to the Word dictionary to make it more comprehensive.

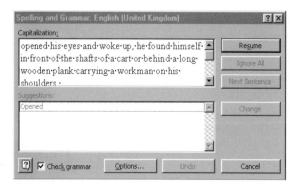

Figure 2.13: Using the Spelling Checker on your text

As for Ménalque, which is an old French proper name, it is up to you to decide whether or not you want to add it to your Word dictionary. If you have no further interest in this word, simply click on the Ignore button.

If you have inserted more than one space between two words the Spelling Checker immediately detects the error and asks if you wish to Replace. When you confirm this command by clicking on the Replace button, the extra space disappears.

SAVE OR SAVE AS

Choosing a drive

When you have finished typing and have corrected your text, you must save your work and store it in a directory or even in a folder. Should it be Drive C or D? Let's assume you opt for Drive C. You must now create the directory on the C drive.

1. Open Windows Explorer

Figure 2.14: Click on Windows Explorer

2. In Windows Explorer, select Drive C.

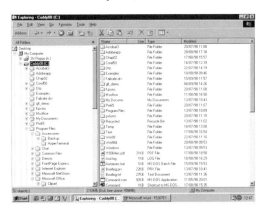

Figure 2.15: Select Drive C

Choosing a directory

1. When you have selected Drive C, open the File menu.

2. Click on the New command.

3. Select the File option.

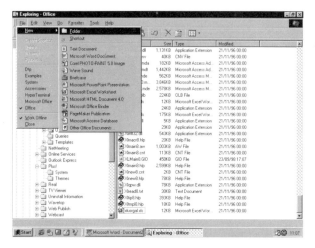

Figure 2.16: Creating a new file

Now all you have to do is enter the chosen name in the text panel.
Talking of names, what do you want to call your La Bruyère file?
Here again, choose a name which is as relevant and descriptive
as possible. Let's assume you've chosen the name 'Dictation':
your directory immediately moves to its alphabetical sequence in
the directory tree of Drive C.

▄▄▄▄ Choosing a folder

If you want to be really methodical, you can also create a folder and give it a name. Say you have opted for the name '17th'. All you have to do now is store your file in this folder.

Select the File menu, click on the Save As command while selecting Folder 17th, which is stored in the Dictation directory on your C hard drive.

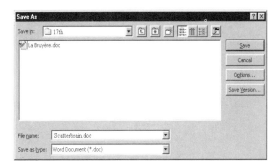

Figure 2.17: Folder '17th' is stored in the Dictation directory on your C hard drive

It is advisable to repeat the Save operation every five to ten minutes in order to avoid losing all the work you have done since the previous save.

1. Open the File menu.

2. Click on the Save or the Save As option. You can also click on the Save icon, which is in the form of a diskette.

3. By clicking on the Save As option in the File menu, you then reveal the Save As dialog box and its options.

To begin with, the text is assigned a default name. In this case, it is Document1. When it is saved for the first time, a series of options is displayed. These options are then applied by default to all subsequent saves. Thus, it is only necessary to click once on the Save icon. To return to the options available during the first save, you must move to the Save As command.

Giving the file a name

So far, your file only has a default name. It is called Document1.

It is advisable to give it a more accurate name in order to avoid any confusion. Over a period of time, a large number of files called Document1, Document2, Document3, Document4 and so forth will become incomprehensible.

Word automatically numbers new documents in sequence (Document1, Document2, etc.) and maintains this numbering sequence even if the previous document has been closed.

1. Choose a suitable name for your file – The Scatterbrain, for example.

2. Open the File menu.

3. Select the Save As command.

4. In the text panel at the bottom of the dialog box, type the chosen name–The Scatterbrain. Word 97 adds the extension .doc.

Figure 2.18: Save your document under the name of your choice

To recap, to save your document, use the following path:

C:\Dictation\17th\The Scatterbrain.

That concludes your second hour.

You now know how to type text, amend it, spellcheck it, give it a name and store it in a folder. You have just created your first document.

Hour 3

Producing a layout

THE CONTENTS FOR THIS HOUR

- Aligning text
- Setting indents
- Cutting text
- Applying Borders and Shading
- Numbering paragraphs
- Choosing a font
- Adding effects to the text
- Choosing the size of the margins
- Defining headers and footers
- Displaying the current page and the total number of pages
- Applying the date and time to the document

When you format a document, you are not only applying current standards of layout, you are also personalising it. It is rather like giving it a particular style. To do this, a number of parameters must be taken into consideration: aligning the text, positioning indents, finding a suitable font, adding page breaks, headers and footers, selecting an original border and embellishing the text with a couple of dropped caps. There is no shortage of ideas.

ALIGNING TEXT

You can align the text of a document on the left or on the right, you can centre it or you can even justify it. Left alignment is the default format used by Word 97. These four types of alignment are represented by the following four icons situated on the Format Toolbar.

Figure 3.1: You have a choice of four types of alignment

- Text aligned on the left is lined up along the left-hand margin, while the right-hand edge is ragged. You can use this layout for private correspondence, for example, where a degree of licence is acceptable.

- Text aligned on the right is lined up along the right-hand margin, while the left-hand edge is ragged. This type of alignment is suitable for formatting lists or for numbering pages.

- Centred text is irregular on both sides. This is the ideal layout for headings, as well as for poetry.

- Justified text is lined up with both the left-hand and right-hand margins. This neat layout is best for official letters and documents.

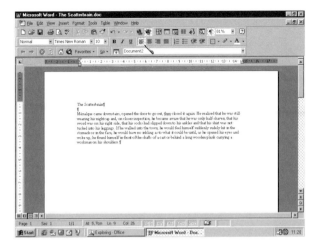

Figure 3.2: The icons used to set the text alignment

SETTING INDENTS

You can easily create indents with the ruler. It contains indent markers in the form of small triangles. You can move them to the right and left along your ruler.

The negative indent moves the first line of an indented paragraph to the left in order to make it stand out from the rest of the paragraph. Negative indents are mainly used for numbered paragraphs, bulleted list, entries in bibliographies and lists in curricula vitae.

Be careful not to confuse paragraph indentation with the definition of the left or right margins! The indentation of a paragraph is a question of the distance between the text and the margins, whereas the parameters defined for margins relate to the overall width of the text.

Changing the first line indent

The small, downward-pointing triangle on the graduated ruler is the
marker for the first line indent. The indent can be moved to the left
(negative indent) or to the right (positive indent).

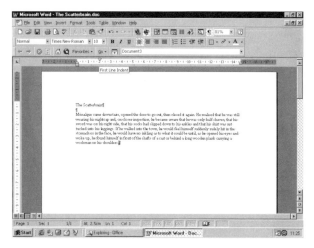

Figure 3.3: Your text with a first line indent

Changing the paragraph indent

The small, upward-pointing triangle on the graduated ruler is the
paragraph indent marker.

Another way of achieving the same result is to open the Format
menu, select the Paragraph option and then click on the Indents and
Spacing tab.

Figure 3.4: Your text with a paragraph indent

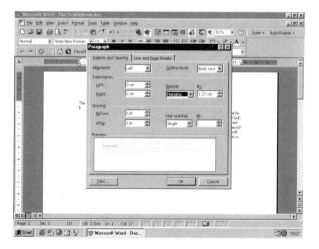

Figure 3.5: The Paragraph dialog box on the Indents and Spacing tab with a paragraph indent

Cutting text

Few things are more unattractive than a text consisting of two pages with just one line on the second page – a widow.

Avoiding widows and orphans

The Widow/Orphan control option is on the Line and Page Breaks tab of the Format menu. This option is used to ensure that the text flows smoothly.

Keeping lines together

Still in the context of formatting, the Keep lines together option holds the lines of a paragraph together.

Let's assume that your paragraph is 20 lines long and available space on the page is only 10 lines: if the Keep lines together option is activated, the entire paragraph will be carried over to the next page.

To locate this option, open the Format menu, select the Paragraph sub-menu, click on the Line and Page Breaks tab and tick the box against Keep lines together.

Keeping paragraphs together

The Keep with next option suppresses a page break after a paragraph. This function is particularly useful in the case of a diagram and its caption, which should not be separated.

Applying Borders and Shading

There are many ways of using Borders and Shading. You can place borders around pages, add them to text, place them around characters to bring them into relief, or add them to graphics and tables; you

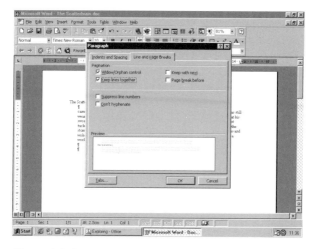

Figure 3.6: The Keep lines together box of the Paragraph dialog box

can also create a shaded background with the colour of your choice. All this adds to the professional appearance of your format. Make sure you don't overdo it – you can have too much of a good thing!

Borders

To apply a border to a complete text or paragraph by paragraph, in the Format menu select the Borders and Shading option.

In addition to the standard borders, other types are available:

- Shadow

- 3-D

- Custom, etc.

There are also different styles of border:

- Continuous lines
- Dashed lines

There is a choice of 22 types of line, with 9 different thicknesses and 8 colours.

The Scatterbrain

> Ménalque came downstairs, opened the door to go out, then closed it again. He realised that he was still wearing his nightcap and, on closer inspection, he became aware that he was only half-shaven, that his sword was on his right side, that his socks had slipped down to his ankles and that his shirt was not tucked into his leggings. If he walked into the town, he would feel himself suddenly rudely hit in the stomach or in the face, he would have no inkling as to what it could be until, as he opened his eyes and woke up, he found himself in front of the shafts of a cart or behind a long wooden plank carrying a workman on his shoulders. He had once been seen to collide with a blind man, getting tangled up with his legs and each of them falling over backwards.

Figure 3.7: A border applied to a paragraph

Shading

A background tint or a colour can be applied at any time to a selected paragraph. Various combinations of colours and motifs can be placed in the background and foreground. In the example shown below, we have chosen a 40% grey tint.

Figure 3.8: A grey tint applied to the selected paragraph

NUMBERING PARAGRAPHS

The bulleted or numbered list functions make it very easy to generate lists:

1. Type the list without entering numbers.

2. Select the list.

3. Click the Bullets icon on the Formatting Toolbar.

To change the symbol to be used (even retroactively):

1. Open the Format menu.

2. Click on the Bullets and Numbering command.

3. Select the Bulleted tab in the Bullets and Numbering dialog box.

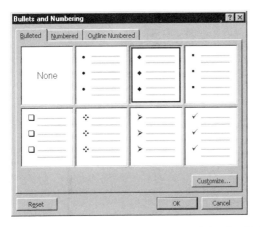

Figure 3.9: Click on the Bulleted tab in the Bullets and Numbering dialog box and choose a bulleted format

You can also choose a Numbers format and make the suggested adjustments.

You can renumber a list by clicking on the button a second time. The lists can also be used in the cells of a table.

The procedures and settings are identical to those employed for the numbers; however, it is possible to choose any character in any of the available fonts.

CHOOSING A FONT

With Windows 95, you have access to TrueType fonts. The advantage of these fonts is that they are displayed on the screen exactly as they will be printed. They can be printed using any printer. You can identify a TrueType font by the 'TT' symbol displayed at the left of each font.

The default font – Times New Roman – is suitable for standard layouts. It can be applied to new documents created using the active template. It is not necessarily the most attractive. Depending on the context of the document, one font may be more suitable than another.

Selecting a font

You can either choose from the Format menu and the Font option or from the scrolling list of fonts in the Toolbar.

You can choose the font either before or after you type the text. The first method is more logical.

1. Open the Format menu.

2. Click on the Font option.

3. Select the Font tab from the Font dialog box.

4. Scroll the list of fonts.

5. Click on the one you want.

6. Confirm by pressing the OK button.

Changing a font

To change a font, use the menu or the Toolbar. The procedure is the same as when you originally chose the font: select your text and then use the Formatting Toolbar or the Format menu.

Enlarging or reducing the font size by one point

- The Enlarge font by one point icon on the Formatting Toolbar enlarges the size of the text font by one point.

- The Reduce font by one point icon on the Formatting Toolbar reduces the size of the text font by one point.

ADDING EFFECTS TO THE TEXT

The simple way

The easy way to add effects to a text is to proceed as follows:

1. Open the Edit Menu.

2. Click on the Select All option. Your text is now selected.

3. Open the Format menu.

4. Select the Font option.

5. Click on the Font tab in the Font dialog box.

6. Select one of the Effects options, such as:

- Bold

- Bold italic

- Italic

- Underline

The elaborate way

More elaborate techniques can also be applied to add effects to a text, such as placing text in relief, adding capital letters and combining different effects with each other. To access these options, the procedure is the same as for the more straightforward effects:

1. Open the Format menu.
2. Click on the Font option.
3. Select the Font tab in the Font dialog box.
4. Tick the text effects box in the Effects box.

Dropped capitals

To insert a dropped capital in place of the first capital letter of your text, proceed as follows:

1. Select the first capital letter of your text.
2. Open the Format menu.
3. Click on the Drop Cap option.
4. Click on the Dropped option.
5. Confirm by pressing OK.

Your selected capital letter is formatted as a dropped capital.

The dropped capital is usually the first letter of a paragraph and may be shown in the left margin or displaced downward in relation to the baseline of the first line of the paragraph.

Figure 3.10: The Drop Cap dialog box in the Format menu

▬▬ Change Case

Changing the case means moving from uppercase to lowercase and vice-versa. To change case, you must do the following:

1. Open the Format menu.

2. Select the Change Case command.

3. Tick the case(s) that you require in the Change Case dialog box.

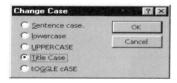

Figure 3.11: The Change Case dialog box in the Format menu

You can also apply the Caps or Small Caps effects throughout the text.

Font effects

- Strikethrough: puts a line through the text.

- Double strikethrough: puts a double line through the selected text.

- Outline: puts a thick outline around the characters.

- Shadow: gives the effect of a shadow against the characters.

- Engrave: gives an engraved (recessed) effect to the characters.

- Small Caps: formats the selected text by replacing lowercase letters with small capital letters. The Small Caps attribute does not affect numerals, punctuation, non-alphabetical characters or characters which are already capital letters.

- Emboss: gives an embossed (raised) effect to the characters.

The Highlight option highlights the text to make it stand out from the surrounding adjacent text. Click on the Highlight icon, then select the text or object to be highlighted. Once the highlight is in place, click on Highlight once again. To change the highlighting colour, click on the arrow to select the colour of your choice.

CHOOSING THE SIZE OF THE MARGINS

Before you print your text, it is a good idea to preview it. In this way, you will be able to see exactly how your document will look once it has been printed.

1. Open the View menu.

2. Select Print Preview. An even easier way is to just click on the icon representing a sheet of paper and a magnifying glass.

3. The left-hand, right-hand, top and bottom margins are displayed.

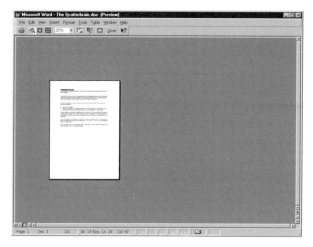

Figure 3.12: The Print Preview and the magnifier cursor

Print Preview lets you see at once if the text is too high. You must then change the top margin.

4. Click on the top margin.

5. Your cursor turns into a bi-directional yellow arrow, which you can use to adjust the size of the margin as required.

You can also alter the page margins by changing to Page Layout view.

1. Click on a margin limit.

2. Proceed when the cursor changes into a bi-directional yellow arrow.

DEFINING HEADERS AND FOOTERS

To perform this operation, proceed as follows:

1. Open the View menu.

2. Select the Header and Footer option. A text area known as the Header appears first. You can enter any information you wish in this panel, such as the subtitle to this document.

3. Enter the subtitle Test 01.

4. Then switch from Header to Footer.

This will display the foot of the page where, for example, you can enter the page numbers and/or the date, time, etc.

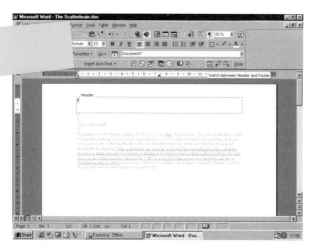

Figure 3.13: Switch from the header area to the footer area

DISPLAYING THE CURRENT PAGE NUMBER AND THE TOTAL NUMBER OF PAGES

This function is particularly useful when you are producing documents which run to several tens of pages, such as reports or novels.

To display the current page number and the total number of pages, proceed as follows:

1. Open the View menu.

2. Click on Header and Footer. The header is displayed.

3. Click the Switch Between Header and Footer icon.

4. Move to the footer.

5. Open the Insert AutoText list.

6. Select the option Page X of Y. If your document is 2 pages long, the footer for page 1 will show Page 1 of 2. All you have to do is centre the pagination.

Figure 3.14: Insert AutoText – Page X of Y

The page numbers are automatically updated when you add or delete pages.

APPLYING THE DATE AND TIME TO THE DOCUMENT

This is an important function, as it indicates the last time the document was revised.

The method used is similar to that already used for pagination.

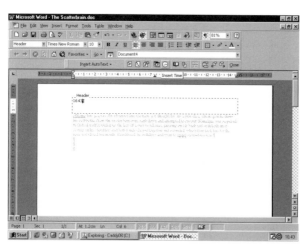

Figure 3.15: The Insert Time icon inserts a time field which is updated automatically

1. Open the View menu.

2. Click on the Header and Footer option.

3. Switch to either the footer or the header.

4. Click on the Insert Time icon, which is in the form of a clock. The time is inserted automatically.

5. Click on the Insert Date icon, which is in the form of two
   sheets of a calendar. The date is inserted automatically.

Then, still in the footer, click on the calendar icon to obtain the
day's date.

Hour 4

Creating style sheets and templates

THE CONTENTS FOR THIS HOUR

- Choosing a style sheet
- Creating a style sheet
- Modifying a style sheet
- Importing styles from another document
- The AutoFormat command
- Printing the styles
- Choosing a template
- Creating a template
- Adding macro commands

Choosing a style sheet

You have just typed a document which is about 200 pages long. You used the Times New Roman font, with double-line spacing and one line between paragraphs, with headings in 14-point italic. You have been advised that it would be better to use the Arial font, with single line spacing and two lines space between paragraphs, with bold but not italic headings.

This means you have to change everything! In a 200-page document, this could prove very time-consuming. The style sheet makes it possible to perform the operation in just a few minutes.

What is a style sheet?

A style sheet consists of a set of styles located in a scrolling list box which is used for highly specific editorial types. It memorises all the characteristics of a paragraph (enhanced layout, alignment, borders, characters, etc. under a single assigned name). Applying a precise style to a paragraph automatically endows it with all the attributes of this style.

For example, different styles may be used for the caption to an illustration, for the main body of text, for an official letter, a personal letter, an invoice or a book.

Let us suppose you have just written the following letter in the normal way. The structure of your letter consists of the company name, the reference, the date, the text and the signature.

A. N. Other
22 Craven Street
Hemel Hempstead
Hertfordshire

26 January 1999

Re: Conference on 19 February 1999

Dear Sir or Madam,

Further to my telephone conversation with Paolo Tardi, may I ask you to give a mobilisation conference in preparation for 9 March, on 19 February in Strasbourg?

The conference will open the Tibet Information Week from 19 February to 1 March, which is to be held at the Tchan Centre, 14 rue des oeillets, 67000 Strasbourg.

Would it be possible to invite one or two Members of the European Parliament to address the conference?

We will be starting to mobilise the local authorities over the next few days.

I look forward to hearing from you.

Yours faithfully

David Harrison
President of the Association

This letter consists of 10 groups of text:

- the address of the addressee,
- the date,
- the reference,
- the text itself, comprising 6 paragraphs and the salutation,
- the signatory's name and position.

The 7 sections of the body of text are in an identical format.

The other 4 parts are in different formats.

You are now going to create suitable styles for these 7 different sections. The final format will be known as the style sheet. Once you have created your style sheet, when you write a new letter all you have to do is apply one of the styles to each new paragraph.

If you then wish to make changes to your letter at a later stage, all you need to do is modify a style and all the paragraphs in this style will be modified automatically.

CREATING A STYLE SHEET

To create a style sheet, you must assign settings to each style, that is give it a structure and name.

Using the Toolbar

1. Select the address

2. Click on the Style box situated at the left-hand edge of the Formatting toolbar.

This box contains a scrolling list of style names. The default settings are Normal, Heading 1, Heading 2, Heading 3, HyperText Link and Default Paragraph Font.

Figure 4.1: The scrolling list of styles

3. In the text panel, type the name you wish to assign to the address, for example Ad. From then on, all you have to do is apply Ad to a section of text in order to ensure that its font, size and position on the page will always be the same.

4. Proceed in the same way for the other elements of the letter.

▄▄▄ Using the dialog box

1. Select the element of the letter to which you want to assign a style.

2. Open the Format menu.

3. Select Style. A dialog box appears on the screen. This contains a list of the styles included in your letter. The style you have just created is also displayed.

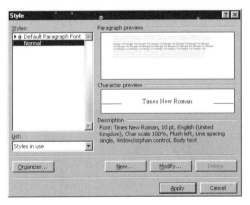

Figure 4.2: The Style dialog box

4. Click on new. A new dialog box appears on the screen.

5. In the text panel marked Name, type the new name you wish to assign to the style. Let us assume that the name is Signature. The Description panel indicates the characteristics of the selected paragraph.

6. If you want to change these characteristics, click on Format and select Characters.

7. Instead of Normal, specify Bold, for example.

8. Confirm by clicking on OK. The dialog box is displayed again.

In the dialog box

- New allows you to create a new style.

- Modify allows you to change an existing style.

- Delete allows you to delete a style.

- Apply allows you to apply a style.

The Style icon, indicated by a double 'A', defines or applies a combination of formats to a selection.

MODIFYING A STYLE SHEET

A style repair and renovation tool is available in order to improve, perfect or polish up a style sheet. To access this tool, click on Format, then Style (Format/Style) once the sheet acting as a template has been activated. The dialog box which appears allows you to select the styles one by one and to adjust any of their components.

To create a number of signature styles – in Engraved or Embossed form, for example – proceed as follows:

1. Position the insertion point on the word 'signature'.

2. Press Ctrl + Shift + S.

3. Assign a name (Signature 1).

4. Repeat the operation several times with Signature 2, 3 and 4.

5. Click on Format/Style in the toolbar. You will then have access to a range of similar styles which you are going to modify.

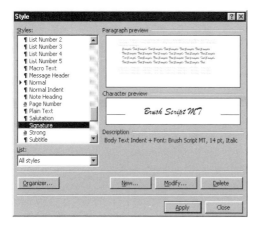

Figure 4.3: The choice of style applied to the signature

To modify, all you need to do is click on the style of your choice.

Figure 4.4: The dialog box used to modify the style

You will note that certain styles are constructed by placing one template on top of another.

Figure 4.5: Preview different styles before changing them

Any modification to a parent style template is reflected in the child templates. Activate the command buttons. Don't forget to tick the option boxes which ensure that the modifications are incorporated into the template and are automatically updated. Exit from the last window by clicking on Apply. The result is that the user is offered a variety of choices of signature.

A style has been modified in an unexpected manner. Check that Automatic Update is activated for the style used. If this is the case, the style is updated when you apply modifications to it, which maintains the cohesion of the elements of your document, such as headings. To deactivate this function, open the Format menu and click on Style. In the Styles panel, click on the style in question, then on Apply. If the Automatic Update tickbox is active, deactivate it.

IMPORTING STYLES FROM ANOTHER DOCUMENT

To import styles which have been applied to another document, proceed as follows:

1. Open the Format menu.

2. Select the Style option.

3. Click on the Organizer button.

4. Choose the file containing the styles to be copied.

5. Copy.

6. Rename the styles (glossaries, menus, macros).

THE AUTOFORMAT COMMAND

The Autoformat command displays a preview of the format of a document based on the styles of a template selected in the Template box.

To select other templates, proceed as follows:

1. Click on the styles you require.

2. Confirm by clicking on OK.

The predefined style of your choice is applied to your letter.

The Autoformat command lets you customise the appearance of your document with the aid of styles originating from other documents.

PRINTING THE STYLES

To print your style sheet as you have just defined it, proceed as follows:

1. Open the File menu.

2. Click on Print.

3. In the Print what: line, select the Styles option.

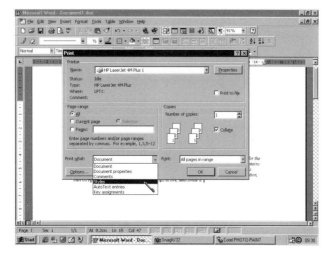

Figure 4.6: Printing the styles

Choosing a template

The style sheet must be formatted by copying the styles.

The other solution is to use a template, in which you only need to type the text and save it under another name.

What is a template?

A template is a document which has been saved in a predefined format. To apply a sheet of standard styles to a document, follow these steps:

1. Open the File menu.

2. Click on New.

3. Choose a template.

4. Click on the Create New Document option.

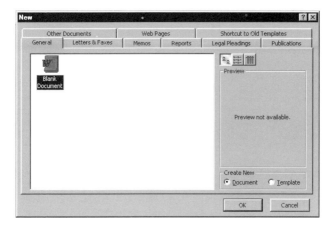

Figure 4.7: Under Create New, activate the Document radio button

Before moving on to Edit, check the different styles displayed on the sheet.

1. Open the box of styles situated at the left-hand side of your Formatting toolbar, then write a word or phrase of your choice.

2. Click on a style name, which will be applied automatically to your word or phrase.

You can scroll through all the standard templates provided by Microsoft. They are normally located in the C:\program files\Microsoft Office\Templates folder, with the extension '.dot'. You can access this folder by clicking on the New command in the File menu.

The tabs offer a range of templates, sorted by category. The list of templates can be displayed in a number of ways:

- Icons

- Lines

- Detailed lines

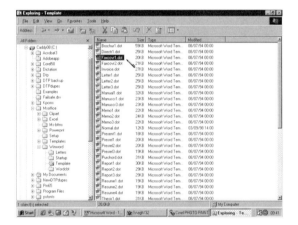

Figure 4.8: The range of Microsoft Office templates

The Templates and Add-Ins option in the Tools menu attaches another template to the active document, loads add-ins or updates the styles of a document. This command also loads additional templates in the form of global templates, to enable you to use their macros, their automatic insertions and the settings for their customised commands.

CREATING A TEMPLATE

If you are asked to produce a precise piece of work, you will be able to create a personalised style sheet. In the following example you will be creating a personalised letter template, albeit one containing only simple elements.

To create a style sheet, proceed as follows:

1. Open the File menu.

2. Select New.

3. Click on the General tab.

4. Select the Blank Document file.

5. Under Create New, tick the Template radio button.

This is how the sheet appears once it has been edited. In practice, you need to complete the work by inserting the name, address and telephone number at the bottom of the page.

Figure 4.9: Create your own template

When you have completed the work, you must save it and give it a name with the extension '.dot'. To improve the template, you can insert styles:

1. In the .dot document, move to an element whose style you wish to preserve.

2. Press Ctrl + Shift + S.

3. A new text appears, in Selection mode. Give it any name you wish. For example, in Figure 4.10, we have chosen the names contained in the text and we have added an Imprint style. It is also possible to add a range of styles to vary the signatures.

ADDING MACRO COMMANDS

Once it has been created and stored in the library, the sheet is a template which can be accessed by any of the users of the PC. It contains fully prepared layout elements, styles and text elements: addressee, place and date, signatures and address/telephone number.

It can be further enhanced by adding macro commands. For example, you are now going to create a library of signatures generated with WordArt, or even personalised page headers and footers.

The first step is to become familiar with WordArt so that you have a clearer idea of what you want to achieve. Once the desired result has been defined, simply proceed as follows:

1. From View/Toolbars/WordArt, activate the WordArt Toolbar.

2. Click on Tools/Macros/Record New Macro.

3. Specify a short name, for example S1 for 'Signature 1'.

4. Specify the availability of this macro (everywhere or only in this style sheet).

5. Start the macro.

6. Click on the blue A icon.

7. Create the signature of your choice (for WordArt, refer to Hour 7).

8. Complete the save.

9. Repeat this operation a number of times in order to obtain a varied choice of original signatures, called S1, S2, S3, etc.

Figure 4.10: Create your first macro

The style sheets can be as numerous and effective as you wish. They can be adapted to the majority of situations. Enhanced with macro commands, they create a complete environment.

To learn how to program macros in Visual Basic 5, begin by creating a simple macro. Then click on Options/Macro and select the one you have just created. Click on the Modify command. You will then see how Word 97 has coded the instructions executed during the save operation.

Hour 5

Improving the text

THE CONTENTS FOR THIS HOUR

- Finding a word and replacing it with another
- Using automatic correction
- Spelling and grammar
- Finding synonyms
- Creating your own dictionary
- Using AutoText
- Compiling statistics
- Requesting an automatic summary
- Using the Letter Wizard
- Inserting a comment
- Tracking changes

Word 97

FINDING A WORD AND REPLACING IT WITH ANOTHER

Let us assume that you have mistakenly used one term instead of
another at 10 locations in the text. Rather than delete this term 10
times and replace it 10 times with the correct term, use the Find
and Replace function. Let us suppose that in our text 'The
Scatterbrain' we need to replace 'he' by the first name 'Ménalque'
in every case. The procedure is as follows:

1. Open the Edit menu.

2. Click on the Replace option.

3. Select the Replace tab.

4. In the Find and Replace dialog box, type the word you want to
   find and replace ('he') in the Find what: text panel.

Figure 5.1: The Find and Replace dialog box

5. Type the replacement word ('Ménalque') in the Replace with:
   text panel.

6. Confirm by clicking on the Replace All button.

Throughout your text, every 'he' will replaced by 'Ménalque'.

USING AUTOMATIC CORRECTION

Word 6 introduced the concept of auto-correction and Word 97
has perfected it. The AutoCorrect function in the Tools menu allows
the user to correct the text automatically as it is being typed.

Let us assume you have written a report covering several pages in which the title 'International Institute of Human Rights' appears at least 10 times. Suppose also you tend to transpose certain letters such as typing 'puls' instead of 'plus'. Before you start typing your report, make a few preparations. Open a document, which you could call 'Error 01' for example, and type the two terms in question:

• The International Institute of Human Rights

• Plus

1. Begin by selecting The International Institute of Human Rights.

2. Open the Tools menu.

3. Click on AutoCorrect.

You can see that incorrectly typed words are listed in the left-hand column and their correct spellings are shown in the right-hand column.

4. Type 'IIHR' in the left-hand column and 'The International Institute of Human Rights' in the right-hand column.

As you type your text, every time you type the abbreviation 'IIHR' it is replaced by the full title 'The International Institute of Human Rights'. This is a real real time-saver! Repeat this operation with 'plus' and any other words you have a tendency to mistype.

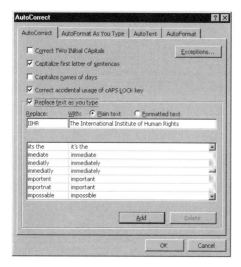

Figure 5.2: Replacing text as you type

Completing a word automatically

The AutoComplete function reduces the time taken to type a word, by offering automatically to complete the last letters of the days of the week, the months of the year and the last numbers of the current date.

The month of Octo|
October|

Figure 5.3: The word 'October' is completed automatically

Let us take the example of 'Saturday', which has eight letters. Once you have typed the 4th letter, the word 'Saturday' appears in full. You need only to press Enter to confirm and the word is completed in the text. If you include the Enter keystroke, you have saved 3 keystrokes; rather than continuing to type 'r', 'd', 'a' and 'y', simply press Enter.

The Resume button in the Spelling Checker selects the next spelling error in the active document.

SPELLING AND GRAMMAR

Word 97 has various features for automatic checking of spelling and grammar. To make use of these features proceed as follows:

1. Open the Tools menu.

2. Select Spelling and Grammar.

3. Click on the Options button.

4. Tick the various checkboxes as required.

More specific grammar settings can then be accessed by clicking on Settings... and ticking the appropriate checkboxes.

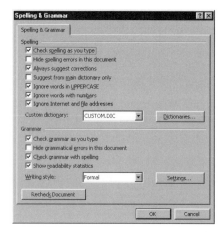

Figure 5.4: Automatically checking spelling and grammar

FINDING SYNONYMS

Word 97 is equipped with a dictionary of synonyms.

1. Select the word for which you want to find a synonym, for example 'adorable'.

2. Open the Tools menu.

3. Click on the Language option.

4. Select Synonyms. A dialog box opens containing a choice of four synonyms for the word 'adorable', based on a standard dictionary. The meaning of the word 'adorable' is shown in the left column. Choose the word you wish to use in place of 'adorable'.

5. Click on the Replace button.

You also have the option of initiating a search for a word of your choice. The dictionary shows you synonyms and meanings.

Let us assume that you are looking for a synonym for scatterbrain.

6. Type 'Scatterbrain' in the text panel.

7. Click on Look Up and the dictionary suggests one synonym.

Figure 5.5: The synonym for scatterbrain

CREATING YOUR OWN DICTIONARY

The spelling checker compares the terms in your text with the terms in its dictionary, which contains thousands of commonly used terms. It is likely that some of the words and expressions you have used do not appear in this lexicon; in particular, this applies to technical terms employed in your profession. You can create custom dictionaries, which the spelling checker will consult with each correction.

How is it done?

1. Open the Tools menu.

2. Choose Options.

3. Click on the Spelling and Grammar tab.

4. Click on the Dictionaries command button.

5. Click the New button in the Custom Dictionaries section.

In the filename panel, assign a name to your dictionary – Mondico, for example.

Figure 5.6: The Custom Dictionaries dialog box

The access path to your new dictionary is:

C:\Program Files\Shared files\Microsoft\Shared\Proof\Mondico.dic

USING AUTOTEXT

The Insert toolbar offers you a choice of elements that you can insert in your document, such as private or professional correspondence letters. Click on the location where you wish to place the AutoText.

Using the Insert menu

1. Open the Insert menu.

2. Select the AutoText submenu.

You are now offered a choice of expressions to be inserted concerning functions, mailing criteria, references, signatures, salutation, etc.

3. Click on the expression which is most appropriate for your letter and it will be inserted automatically. You can modify these elements at any time.

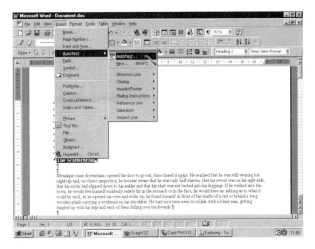

Figure 5.7: The range of AutoText options

Using the Toolbar

The AutoText icon on the Insert toolbar allows you to call up the elements you wish to insert, modify or delete.

COMPILING STATISTICS

This function is particularly useful if you are working with people who assess texts by the number of characters (including punctuation and spaces). This is the case with the majority of texts for periodicals, weekly journals, reviews, magazines, etc.

Suppose for a given typeface and type size a page contains 1,500 characters. As you are typing your text, you can check the number of characters and spaces at any time. To do this:

1. Select the text.

2. Open the File menu.

3. Click on the Properties option.

4. Activate the Statistics tab.

'The Scatterbrain' is a text consisting of 5,987 characters, excluding spaces, or, alternatively, 7,180 characters and spaces.

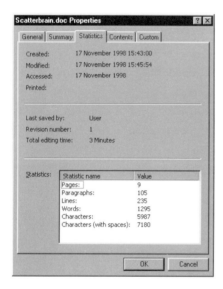

Figure 5.8: Compiling statistics

The Statistics option in the Properties submenu of the File menu counts the number of pages, words, characters, paragraphs and lines in the active document. Punctuation marks and special characters are also included in this calculation.

REQUESTING AN AUTOMATIC SUMMARY

Word 97 will produce a statistical and linguistic analysis of documents. It selects the most important phrases. The AutoSummarize function allows the user to evaluate the contents of the document quickly. The key points of the text are displayed.

To read the document summary online it is necessary to view the document in AutoSummarize mode. This mode provides two options: to display the key points of the text or to display the entire document with the key points highlighted.

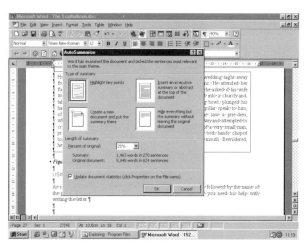

Figure 5.9: AutoSummarize view

Let us now generate an automatic summary of The Scatterbrain.

1. Open the Tools menu.

2. Click on AutoSummarize. The AutoSummarize dialog box is displayed.

3. Select the option Hide everything but the summary without leaving the original document. From our text of 7,180 characters and spaces, the summary of 25% of the text, the key passage is that Ménalque married, forgot about it, buried his wife and remembered nothing more about it.

You can adjust the volume of the summary you wish to see displayed.

Figure 5.10: AutoSummarize applied to 'The Scatterbrain'

USING THE LETTER WIZARD

As soon as you start to type the heading of a letter – 'Dear' for example – followed by the name of the person to whom you are writing, the Letter Wizard asks whether you need his help with writing the letter.

Figure 5.11: The Letter Wizard

1. Type 'Dear Friend'.

2. Confirm by pressing Enter. The Letter Wizard appears and asks you:

   • if you want him to help you write the letter,

   • if you would prefer to type the letter without help.

3. Click on the button Get help with writing the letter.

The Letter Wizard offers you a choice of settings to specify, such as the sender, addressee, the format of the letter, the editorial style, and the layout.

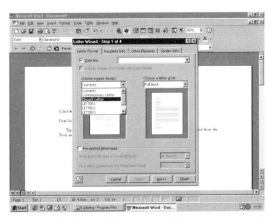

Figure 5.12: Help with writing a letter in an elegant style

If you have not installed the Letter Wizard, you can enlist his aid in the following way:

1. Open the File menu.

2. Click on New.

3. Select the Letters and Faxes tab.

4. Double-click on the Letter Wizard.

INSERTING A COMMENT

You can insert comments concerning your text.

1. Open the Insert menu.

2. Click on the Comment option.

3. Select the word or group of words on which you want to comment.

For example, select the word 'Scatterbrain', which will then be highlighted in yellow.

4. In the text panel which appears at the base of the screen, type the comment you wish to make about your highlighted word.

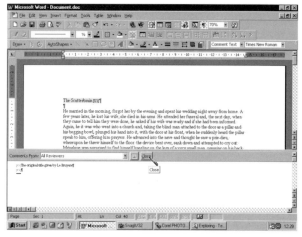

Figure 5.13: Insert a comment at the base of the screen

TRACKING CHANGES

Word 97 allows you to highlight changes. To keep track of changes, proceed as follows:

1. Open the Tools menu.

2. Select the Track Changes option.

Figure 5.14: Choose the modifications which appear on the screen

3. Tick the box Display modifications on the screen. From now on, any modifications applied to your document will appear on the screen.

▬▬▬ Display today's modifications

You can also refine your request. Let us say you want to view the modifications for a given period.

1. Open the Tools menu.

2. Select Track Changes, then the Compare Documents option.

3. Scroll down the Last modified list.

4. Select 'today'.

You have a choice between:

- today

- last week

- this week

- last month

- this month

- any time

5. Click on the Search option and the text panel indicates the number of files which have been modified today.

6. Click on the Open command button in order to open these files. The files which have been modified today are opened.

View Modifications consists of highlighting the changes applied to the content of a shared folder, including the cut or pasted content, and the lines and columns which have been inserted or deleted.

Hour 6

Columns

THE CONTENTS FOR THIS HOUR

- Laying out a document in two columns
- Creating a heading across a number of columns
- Inserting a picture
- Changing the number of columns
- Adding separator lines
- Adjusting the space between the columns
- Adjusting the width of the columns
- Viewing the columns
- Equalising the length of the columns
- Deleting columns
- Enlisting the aid of the Newsletter Wizard

LAYING OUT A DOCUMENT IN TWO COLUMNS

The Columns mode allows the text to be laid out in a number of columns – up to 12 – running in sequence within the same section. There is a correlation between the legibility of the text and the number of columns. A text laid out in columns with an average of 13–14 words per line is easier to read than an unbroken area of text with many more words per line.

Word 97 lets you change the layout of your document into columns. It is possible to lay out the text in two columns on one page and in three columns on another page.

Let us say you want to lay out the text of 'The Scatterbrain' in two columns. To do this:

1. First type the entire text.

2. Place the pointer on the title.

3. Open the Insert menu.

4. Select the Break option.

5. In the Break dialog box, tick the Continuous box under Section Breaks (you do not want a page break).

Figure 6.1: The Break dialog box

6. Move the pointer to the second section of your text.

7. Open the Format menu.

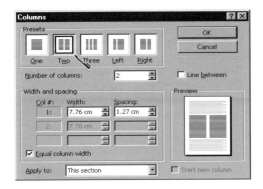

Figure 6.2: In the Columns dialog box, select the Two box

8. Select the Columns option.

9. Click on Two.

If necessary, change to Page Layout View

10. Place the pointer at the end of the first column.

11. Choose Column Break.

Your document is now arranged in 2 columns. You can now apply formatting: justification, hyphenation, etc.

Figure 6.3: Your text is now arranged in two columns

*Word determines the number of columns you can create on
a given page on the basis of three parameters: the width of
the page, the width of the margins and the size and spacing
of the columns.*

CREATING A HEADING ACROSS A NUMBER OF COLUMNS

- If your text is not yet laid out in columns, create the required number of columns.

- In Outline View, select the text which is to form the heading

- Click on Columns, then drag the mouse pointer to select a single column.

INSERTING A PICTURE

To insert a picture in your columns, you must first insert a frame.
To do this:

1. Open the Insert menu.

2. Select the Picture option.

3. Click on AutoShapes.

4. Choose the most suitable shape – Plaque for example.

5. Confirm by pressing Enter. The pointer changes into a yellow cross.

6. Place the pointer in the position where you wish to insert your Plaque shape.

7. Open the Insert menu.

8. Select the Text Box option.

9. Select an illustration from your pictures.bmp files under Format Painter, for example, or the Drawing program supplied with Windows.

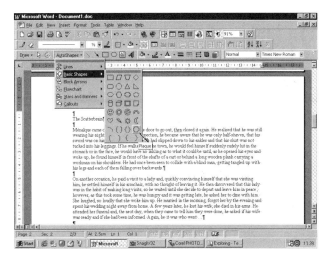

Figure 6.4: Insert the Plaque AutoShape

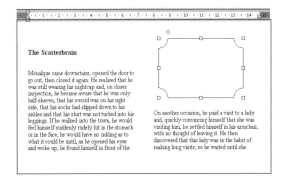

Figure 6.5: The pointer changes into a yellow cross. Position it where you wish to insert the Plaque shape

10. Open the File menu.

11. Click on the Copy option. Your picture is now in the Clipboard.

12. Return to the text of The Scatterbrain.

13. Position the pointer inside the Plaque frame.

14. Open the Edit menu.

15. Select the Paste option.

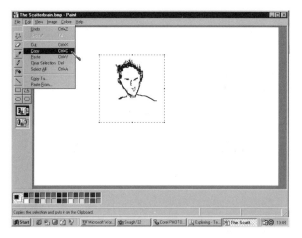

Figure 6.6: Take your drawing, created with the aid of the Format Painter program, and copy it to the Clipboard

Your illustration now appears in the text.

 Format Painter (formerly called Paintbrush) is a program for creating simple images and is adequate for most requirements. It can be used to import and then modify a picture with the Print-Screen command or with the key sequence Alt + Print Screen.

CHANGING THE NUMBER OF COLUMNS

To change the number of columns in your document, the procedure is as follows:

1. Change to Page Layout view.

2. Select the entire document.

3. Open the Edit menu.

4. Click on the Select All option.

5. Open the Format menu.

6. Click on the Columns option.

7. Choose Three.

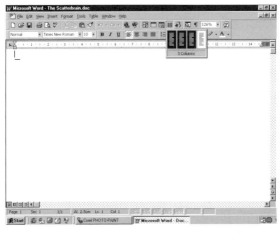

Figure 6.7: The Columns icon allows you to select the number of columns you require

ADDING SEPARATOR LINES

To add separator lines between the columns, change to Page Layout view. If your document is subdivided into sections, proceed as follows:

1. Click in the section to be modified.

2. Open the Format menu.

3. Click on the Columns option.

4. Click on the Line between option.

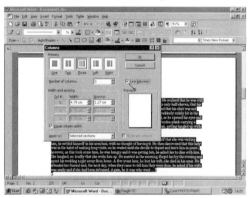

Figure 6.8: The Line between tickbox in the Columns dialog box

ADJUSTING THE SPACE BETWEEN COLUMNS

You can change the space between columns at any time. The default spacing is 1.27 cm. If you want to create a number of columns, reduce this spacing in order to leave more room for the text. You can also increase the column spacing. There are two ways of adjusting the space between columns: by using the Columns dialog box or by using the ruler.

Using the ruler

1. In the View menu, activate the Ruler option. The grey areas on the ruler represent the spacing between the columns.

2. Position the pointer on one of these grey areas. The pointer changes into a bi-directional black arrow.

3. Drag the column marks to increase or reduce the space between the columns in your document. The changes will be applied to all the columns.

Using the Columns dialog box

To adjust the space between the columns using the dialog box, proceed as follows:

1. Position the pointer where you wish to make changes.

2. In the Format menu, select the Columns option.

3. In the Width and spacing section, activate the arrows which adjust the width and spacing.

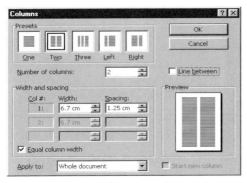

Figure 6.9: The Width and spacing section of the dialog box lets you adjust the space between columns

Adjusting the width of the columns

The procedure for adjusting the width of the columns is more or less the same as that for adjusting the space between the columns.

You can change the width with the aid of the interface, by dragging and dropping on the ruler or by using the Format menu. The widths of the columns can be varied. It is possible to equalise the text between the columns.

Using the ruler

1. Open the View menu.

2. Click on the Ruler option.

3. Position the pointer on the ruler. It then changes into a bi-directional yellow arrow.

4. Drag the column markers to increase or reduce the width of the columns.

Using the Format menu

1. Open the Format menu

2. Choose the Columns option.

3. Activate the column width counter.

If the text within the column is wider than intended you have almost certainly applied a negative indent to the first line of the text. Click in the text, then check the ruler. If an indent marker is to the right or to the left of the column marker, drag it to align it on this column marker.

VIEWING THE COLUMNS

If you are unable to display the newspaper-type columns you have just created, there are two possible explanations. Either your text may not be long enough to carry over into a second column or you may have changed to Normal view.

To display the boundaries of columns, proceed as follows:

1. First, select Page layout view.

2. Then open the Tools menu.

3. Click on Options.

4. Click on the View tab.

5. Activate the Text boundaries check box.

Figure 6.10: Tick the Text boundaries check box in the View tab

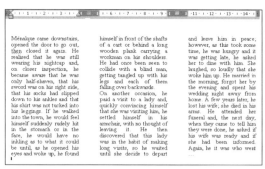

Figure 6.11: The limits of the text appear on the screen

To hide the text, click on the Show/Hide option.

EQUALISING THE LENGTH OF THE COLUMNS

If your text is long and arranged in a number of columns over several pages it is important to ensure that the columns are the same length and width throughout. Word 97 equalises the length of the columns and aligns them automatically.

Nonetheless, a widow or orphan column may still be present in your text. For example, three-and-a-half columns may appear on the same page, as that is where your text ends. The situation can be rectified as follows.

1. Place the insertion point at the end of the text.

2. Open the Insert menu.

3. Select the Break option.

4. Under Section breaks, select Continuous.

5. Confirm with OK.

The length of the columns is equalised by adding a section break at the end of the document.

Do not forget to deactivate the tickbox Don't balance columns for continuous section starts! To find this tickbox, open the Tools menu, select Options and click on the Compatibility tab.

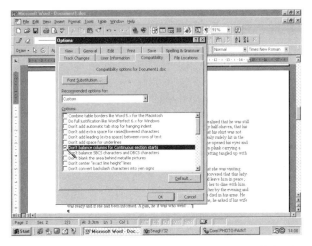

Figure 6.12: The Compatibility tab in the Options dialog box

DELETING COLUMNS

You can delete columns from your document by using the dialog box.

1. Position the insertion point where you wish to make changes.

2. Open the Format menu.

3. Choose the Columns option.

4. To return to a single column click on One in the Predefine group.

ENLISTING THE AID OF THE NEWSLETTER WIZARD

The Newsletter Wizard will compile a newsletter according to your instructions. To enlist his help, proceed as follows:

1. Open the File menu.
2. Click on New.
3. Select the General tab.
4. Click on the Publications tab.

The newsletter is created on the basis of three criteria:

- Style and color: this may be set as professional, contemporary or elegant.
- Title and content: this adds reference to the title, date and volume number.
- Mailing label: if required, this reserves a space at the end of the newsletter for a mailing label.

5. Change from one dialog box to another by clicking on Next.
6. Click on Finish when your mockup is complete.
7. If you click on the Office Companion icon, the Office Companion appears and offers you two types of assistance:

- Help with the Newsletter function.
- Help with something else.

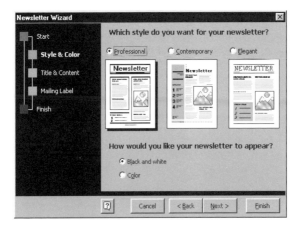

Figure 6.13: The Newsletter Wizard asks you which style to use for your newsletter

Hour 7

Illustrating a document

THE CONTENTS FOR THIS HOUR

- Creating a heading in 3D
- Inserting a WordArt object
- Editing the text
- Changing the colour
- Adjusting the character spacing of a WordArt object
- Adjusting the settings for the WordArt object
- Adjusting the lighting of a WordArt object
- Adding a shadow
- Inserting AutoShapes
- Placing a drawing in the foreground or background
- Typing text to fit around irregular objects
- Creating a customised page border

CREATING A HEADING IN 3D

With WordArt in Word 97, you can add a 3D effect to lines, shapes
and objects using the 3D button on the Drawing toolbar. 3D options
allow you to modify the depth of the drawing as well as its colour,
its angle, the lighting direction and the surface reflection. To modify
the 3D effect of a drawing, click on 3D Settings, then use the tools
on the 3D settings toolbar.

Figure 7.1: The 3D Settings toolbar

The five lighting icons on the 3D Settings toolbar provide
information about:

- the depth,
- the direction,
- the lighting,
- the surface,
- the 3D colour (Automatic).

1. Select your heading – The Scatterbrain.
2. Click on the 3D icon and then on Lighting 3D Settings.
3. Select the Depth option.
4. Set the number of points for the depth you wish to give your
   heading, 72 or 144 points for example.

INSERTING A WORDART OBJECT

You can create headings and texts in 3D by using the WordArt
technique.

To access the WordArt option, proceed as follows:

1. Open the Insert menu.

2. Select the Picture submenu.

3. Click on WordArt.

You can also use the WordArt icon on the Drawing toolbar. This gives you access to 30 types of predefined styles.

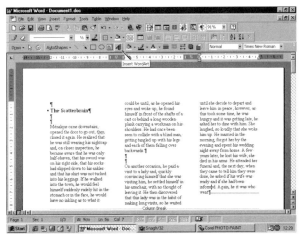

Figure 7.2: The WordArt icon

To create a heading using predefined WordArt styles:

1. Select your heading – The Scatterbrain.

2. Delete it by pressing Ctrl + Del.

3. Move to the position where you want to insert the new heading with WordArt styles.

4. Click on the Insert WordArt icon.

5. Select the WordArt style you wish to use.

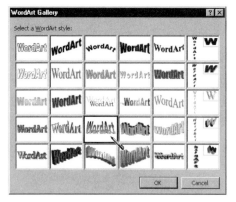

Figure 7.3: Predefined WordArt styles

6. Type your heading in the text box.

7. Set the choice of font and style.

8. Confirm. Your heading then appears with the desired styles. You can rotate this heading in any direction.

9. Select your heading and click on the Free Rotate icon. The pointer changes into a white arrow which points to a circular arrow indicating a rotary movement.

Figure 7.4: The rotation handles are displayed in green with a rounded black arrow

10. Click on this handle to incline your heading.

Figure 7.5: Before the rotation movement

Figure 7.6: After the rotation movement

The WordArt shape option, represented by the Abc icon, allows you to apply to this heading and its new direction any of 40 varied shapes, including:

- Stop,
- Triangle Up,
- Chevron Up,
- Arch Down (Pour),
- Semicircle,
- Deflate,
- Fade,
- Inflate, etc.

1. Click on your 3D heading to activate it.

2. Click on Abc.

3. Then select a shape, for example Ring Inside.

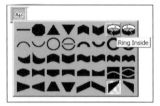

Figure 7.7: The Ring Inside and the other WordArt shapes

Your heading now has a predefined style plus the Ring Inside style.

Figure 7.8: The WordArt shapes allow you to apply a wide variety of twists and turns to your text

EDITING THE TEXT

The Edit Text button on the WordArt toolbar allows you to edit your text at any time without changing the predefined shape. To do this, proceed as follows:

1. Select the WordArt object.

2. Click on the Edit Text button on the WordArt toolbar. The WordArt Edit Text dialog box appears on the screen. You can then change the font, the size and the font style. You can also make any necessary amendments to your text.

The size of a WordArt object

Once it has been inserted into your document, you can adjust the size of your WordArt object. This can range from full page size to a line a few centimetres long.

CHANGING THE COLOUR

You can change the colours of the predefined WordArt objects at any time. Simply click on the Fill Color icon on the Drawing toolbar.

1. Click on the WordArt object you have inserted into the text.

2. Open the Fill Color palette of colours. Use this to add a colour or a style to the selected object. You can also use it to modify or delete the style and the colour. The fill styles include the shade, the texture, the pattern and the picture.

ADJUSTING THE CHARACTER SPACING OF A WORDART OBJECT

You can adjust the character spacing of a WordArt object.

1. Click on the AV icon on the Drawing toolbar to open the Kern Character Pairs submenu.

You can adjust the character spacing of the letters in your object so that they are Very Tight, Tight, Normal, Loose or Very Loose. You can choose Normal spacing.

Normal spacing

Normal spacing automatically adjusts the spacing between certain combinations of characters in order to ensure that the letters in the word are evenly spaced.

This setting only operates with True Type fonts or with the Adobe Type Manager.

ADJUSTING THE SETTINGS FOR THE WORDART OBJECT

You can adjust the settings of the WordArt object. The Format WordArt icon opens the dialog box to allow you to adjust the object settings.

It determines the line style, the colour, the format, the position on the page, the fill colour, etc.

ADJUSTING THE LIGHTING OF A WORDART OBJECT

You are now going to create another heading in 3D and then adjust the lighting.

To do this, proceed as follows:

1. Select the WordArt option.

2. Choose a predefined 3D style.

3. Type The Scatterbrain in the text box.

4. Confirm.

5. Select the object.

6. Click on the Lighting icon on the 3D settings of the Drawings toolbar. You can simultaneously adjust the brightness and direction of the lighting. Begin by adjusting the brightness.

Figure 7.9: Type your text into the WordArt Edit Text dialog box

Three options are available:

- Bright

- Normal

- Dim

7. Click on Lighting/Bright.

The heading has a brighter appearance.

Figure 7.10: The Bright option of the Lighting settings

Figure 7.11: The changed lighting of your 3D heading

This time, you are going to change the direction of the lighting.

You have nine options:

- inclined from the left,
- inclined from the right,
- from below,
- from above,
- central, and so on.

Central lighting provides the brightest illumination of your object.

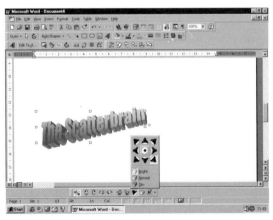

Figure 7.12: You can specify the direction of the lighting

ADDING A SHADOW

You can add a shadow to a shape or to a drawing by using the Shadow tool on the Drawing toolbar.

To adjust the position of the shadow or to change its colour, click on Shadow/ Shadow Settings on the Drawing toolbar.

You can add a shadow or a 3D style, but not both at the same time. If you apply a 3D style to a drawing which already has a shadow, the shadow will disappear.

INSERTING AUTOSHAPES

You can embellish your text at any time by inserting any of the 100 AutoShapes provided by Word 97. To do this, proceed as follows:

1. Either open the AutoShapes list on the Drawing toolbar or open the Insert menu.

2. Select the AutoShapes option. You are offered a choice of six categories of AutoShape:

- Lines

- Basic Shapes

- Block Arrows

- Flowchart

- Stars and Banners

- Callouts

3. Select Callouts.

Figure 7.13: The Cloud Callout on the Callouts option

4. Select the Cloud Callout shape.

5. Position this shape in the required text box.

6. Click on the text box icon. The pointer changes into a yellow cross, which you then move inside the callout.

7. Type your comment inside the callout.

Strip cartoons use the term 'speech bubble' instead of 'callout' and this is a colloquial adaptation of the word 'phylactery', which has its origins in banners bearing inscriptions.

Figure 7.14: Combine the different formatting options for your illustrations

PLACING A DRAWING IN THE FOREGROUND OR BACKGROUND

You can insert any drawing or any AutoShape at any of the three available levels:

- At the same level as the text,
- Behind the text,
- In front of the text.

When it is inserted, the drawing is always in the foreground, placed over the text. If you want to place your drawing in the background, proceed as follows:

1. On the Drawing toolbar, click on Draw
2. Select Order.
3. Click on Bring in Front of Text.

TYPING TEXT TO FIT AROUND IRREGULAR OBJECTS

To type text around irregular objects, proceed as follows:

1. Open the View menu.
2. Select the Toolbars submenu.
3. Click on the Customize option.
4. Select Picture. The Picture toolbar is displayed.
5. Select the Text Wrapping icon.
6. Click the right mouse button when the Text Wrapping submenu is open.
7. Select the Format Text Area option.
8. Click on the Text Wrapping option. You are offered a choice of different text wrapping formats.
9. Select the Top and Bottom option.

Figure 7.15: Top and Bottom text wrapping for an irregular object

10. Now type your text.

11. Cut your illustration.

12. Paste it into the text area.

The text is immediately distributed around the object in the specified manner: Top and Bottom.

Ménalque came downstairs, opened the door to go out, then closed it again. He realised that he

was still wearing his nightcap and, on closer inspection, he became aware that he was only half-shaven, that his sword was on his right side

Figure 7.16: Typing around irregular objects

CREATING A CUSTOMISED PAGE BORDER

Word 97 allows you to apply a customised border to each page. In addition to the 150 new border line styles, Word 97 is supplied with more than 150 artistic border styles originating from the BorderArt product, which is included in Microsoft Publisher.

To access Microsoft Publisher:

1. Open the Format menu.

2. Either select the Borders and Shading submenu or Click on the Outside Border icon on the Tables and Borders toolbar.

To place a border around a paragraph, click anywhere in the paragraph.

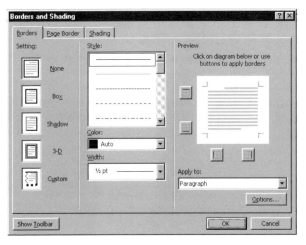

Figure 7.17: Create a customised border

To place a border around a particular piece of text or specific word, select that text or word.

To place a frame around specific sides only, click on Print Preview on the side(s) in question.

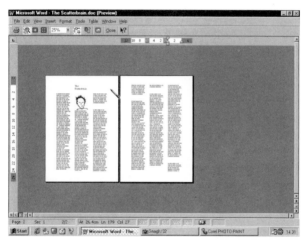

Figure 7.18: Print Preview gives you an idea of the final result

To specify the exact position of the border in relation to the text:

1. Click on Options.
2. Select the required options.

If you want to frame the two pages of your 'Scatterbrain' text and then customise the frame:

1. Click on the Page Border tab.
2. Choose the border you require.

Hour 8

Creating tables

THE CONTENTS FOR THIS HOUR

- Specifying the Office program for creating tables
- Creating a table
- Changing the size of a table
- Improving the layout of a table
- Adding background shading to a table
- Adding a border
- Showing or hiding the gridlines
- Using AutoFormat
- Converting a table to text and vice-versa
- Adding numbers in a row or column

SPECIFYING THE OFFICE PROGRAM FOR CREATING TABLES

It is often necessary to use tables in word-processing. There are various ways of doing this. The first is to use Excel and then insert the table into Word via the Clipboard. This method is recommended if you intend to insert complex calculations, statistical analyses or diagrams into your table. If you want to utilise the Sort, Advanced Search and Relational Database functions, you must use Microsoft Access. Word 97 itself is particularly effective for creating tables containing complex graphics formats, bulleted lists, customised tabs, numbered lists, first line indents, different formats for individual cells or diagonal splitting of the cells.

CREATING A TABLE

Word allows you to create tables composed of rows and columns you can specify yourself. The intersection of a row and a column is called a cell. Inside each cell, you can type numbers, words, phrases, paragraphs, graphics or pictures. Each cell is independent. You can insert your table anywhere in the document and resize it as required. You can automatically add a heading, a caption, an equation or customised borders.

You can also manually add a caption to an existing element:

1. Click on the Insert Table icon in the Standard toolbar.

2. Drag the pointer across and down to obtain the required number of rows and columns. You will need five rows and four columns.

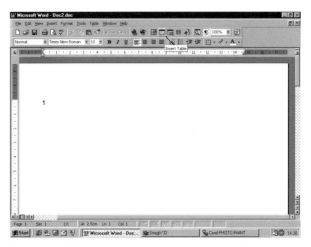

Figure 8.1: Place the pointer on the Insert Table icon

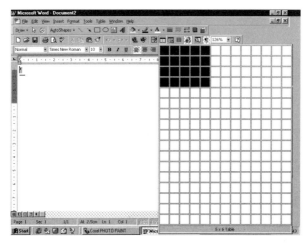

Figure 8.2: Click on the Insert Table icon and create a table to your own requirements

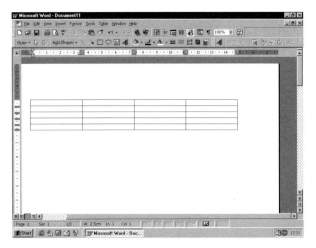

Figure 8.3: The table is inserted into your page

A blank table, consisting of four columns and five rows, is displayed. All the columns are the same width.

The insertion point is situated in the first cell of the first column.

3. Type your text. Enter 'To acquire'. To move to the next column, press Arrow right or Tab.

4. Then type 'I acquire', 'I acquired' and 'acquired'. When you reach the last cell in the row, press Tab to move to the next row.

5. Continue until the table is complete.

▰▰▰ Selecting a cell

To select a cell, click on the selection bar of the cell to the right of the text in the cell. When the pointer is on the bar, it changes into an upward-pointing white arrow.

The cell is selected when its background turns black, i.e. in reverse video.

To acquire	I acquire	I acquired	Acquired
To conclude	I conclude	I concluded	Concluded
To join	I join	I joined	Joined
To hold	I hold	I held	Held
To conquer	I conquer	I conquered	Conquered

Figure 8.4: The selected cell in your table appears in reverse video, i.e. white letters on a black background

Changing the size of a cell

To change the height of a cell:

1. Select the text inside the cell, including the end-of-cell marker.

2. Move the pointer, which is now in the form of two small arrows pointing upward and downward. Drag the cell in a vertical direction (up or down as required).

To change the width of a cell:

1. Select the text inside the cell, including the end-of-cell marker.

2. Move the pointer, which is now in the form of two small arrows pointing to the left and right. Drag the cell in a horizontal direction (left or right as required).

Figure 8.5: Use the interface to change the width of a cell

▬▬▬ Selecting a row

Double-click on the selection bar of a cell. You can also use the Table menu and click on the Select Row option.

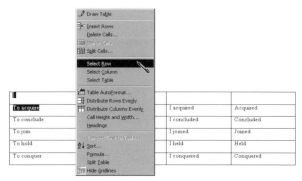

Figure 8.6: Select a row

▬▬▬ Selecting a column

To select a column:

1. Place the pointer at the top of the first cell of the column.

2. Click.

To acquire	I acquire	I acquired	Acquired
To conclude	I conclude	I concluded	Concluded
To join	I join	I joined	Joined
To hold	I hold	I held	Held
To conquer	I conquer	I conquered	Conquered

Figure 8.7: Select a column

You can also use the Table menu and click on the Select Column option.

Figure 8.8: Select a column using the table menu

▬▬▬ Selecting an entire table

To select the entire table, proceed as follows:

1. Click on the last cell at the bottom right of the table.

2. Hold down the mouse button.

3. Move the pointer to the first cell of the table.

You can also use the Table menu and click on the Select Table option.

CHANGING THE SIZE OF A TABLE

A table may change: it can become larger or smaller, depending on the content. This may require frequent modifications, but they can be applied in a straightforward and methodical manner.

▬▬▬ Inserting rows

To insert a row:

1. Place the insertion point in the first cell of the table.

2. Click on the Insert Rows icon.

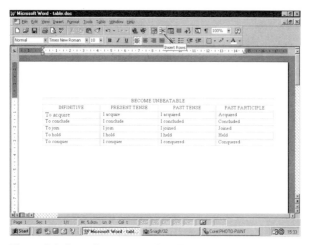

Figure 8.9: Inserting a row using the Insert Rows icon

An extra row is added to the table.

Inserting columns

To insert a column:

1. Place the mouse pointer on the gridline between the two columns. The pointer changes into a black arrow pointing downwards.

2. Click on the Insert Columns icon.

Deleting a row

To delete a row:

1. Select the blank cells in the row you want to delete.

2. Click the right mouse button to display the Table menu.

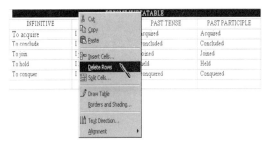

Figure 8.10: Open the Table menu to delete rows

3. Choose the Delete Rows option.

4. Confirm.

Deleting a column

To delete a column:

1. Select the blank cells of the column you want to delete.

2. Click the right mouse button to display the Table menu.

3. Choose the Delete Columns option.

Moving a row

To move a row:

1. Select the row.

2. Place the pointer on the selected row.

3. Move the pointer to the new position.

The row is now in the required position.

Figure 8.11: Use Drag-and-Drop to move a row

Moving a column

To move a column:

1. Select the column.

2. Place the pointer on the selected column.

3. Move the pointer to the new position.

The column is now in the required position.

IMPROVING THE LAYOUT OF A TABLE

Once the table has been designed, it is possible to improve the ease of working. This stage is important, because it means that work can proceed in a convenient manner. Here more than anywhere else the user is working for his or her own convenience.

Tabs

How do you define the tab stops with leaders within your table? Select the column in which you want to incorporate the leader before a tab.

In this case, column 1 of the 1st row to the 5th row.

1. Open the Format menu.

2. Click on Tabs.

3. Under Tab stop position, indicate the position of the new tab, namely 2 cm.

4. Under Alignment, tick the box for the alignment you want to apply to the text.

5. Choose Right.

6. Under Leader, tick the box for the type of leader you wish to use.

7. Confirm.

Figure 8.12: The Tabs dialog box with the Leader option

8. Press Ctrl + TAB. The leaders are displayed in the first column.

To acquire	I acquire
To conclude	I conclude
To join	I join
To hold	I hold
To conquer	I conquer

Figure 8.13: The table with the leaders

You can apply any improvements or modifications you wish, such as:

* Centring the heading

- Changing the colour

- Deleting leaders, etc.

INFINITIVE	PRESENT TENSE	PAST TENSE	PAST PARTICIPLE
To acquire	I acquire	I acquired	Acquired
To conclude	I conclude	I concluded	Concluded
To join	I join	I joined	Joined
To hold	I hold	I held	Held
To conquer	I conquer	I conquered	Conquered

Figure 8.14: The table in its final form

Distributing columns and rows evenly

To distribute the columns evenly, proceed as follows:

1. Select a number of columns.

2. Open the Table menu.

3. Click on Distribute Columns Evenly.

Figure 8.15: Distributing the columns evenly across the table

To distribute the rows evenly, proceed as follows:

1. Select a number of rows.

2. Open the Table menu.

3. Click on Distribute Rows Evenly.

▩▩▩ Merging cells

To insert a heading row and merge the cells:

1. Place the insertion point in the row above the one in which you want to insert a heading row.

2. Open the Table menu.

3. Click on the Insert Rows option.

You then obtain a row divided into four parts which match up with your four columns.

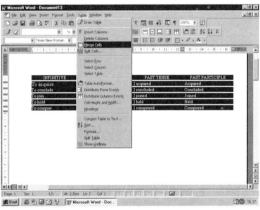

Figure 8.16: Merging cells in your table

4. Select all the cells to be merged.

5. Click on the Merge Cells option.

6. Place the insertion point in the new row, which has not been subdivided.

7. Type your heading.

8. Enhance your text.

9. Centre the text by clicking on the Center icon.

In Word, when you merge cells all the contents of a number of adjacent cells are combined in a single cell. In Excel, merging cells means that the contents of two or more selected cells are combined in a single cell. The reference for a merged cell corresponds to the cell at the upper left-hand corner of the original selection. If you merge a number of cells into one, only the content of the upper left-hand cell is retained.

ADDING BACKGROUND SHADING TO A TABLE

You can refine the appearance of your table by adding background shading to enhance the background of the table, of a paragraph or of selected text. To do this, proceed as follows:

1. Click anywhere in the table.

2. Select the cells where you want the background shading to appear.

3. Open the Format menu.

4. Select the Borders and Shading option.

5. Click on the Shading tab.

6. Choose your colour palette. The background shading may be coloured, clear, dark trellis, light up, down diagonal, etc.

7. Click on the Apply to: list.

8. Confirm by clicking on OK.

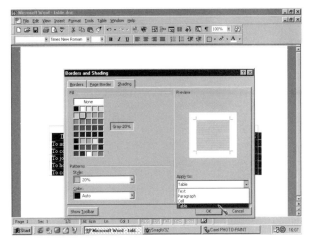

Figure 8.17 Adding background shading to your table

ADDING A BORDER

You can add a border to one or more sides of the table. This border may incorporate a picture, for example a row of trees or a pile of books. You can also embellish your table with an area of text, an AutoShape, a drawing or even an imported picture.

In Word 97, the default setting for tables is a single, continuous black border with a line thickness of ½ point.

To insert a border:

1. Click anywhere in the table.

2. Select the side where you want the border to appear.

3. Open the Format menu.

4. Select the Borders and Shading option.

5. Click on the Borders tab.

6. Design your border. You can choose the type and style of the border, its colour and thickness, as well as the distance from the text.

7. Click on the Apply to: list.

8. Confirm by clicking on OK

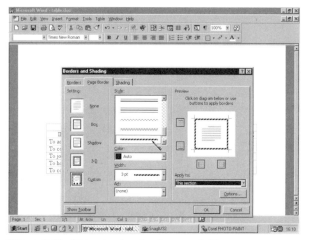

Figure 8.18: Choose a border for your table

SHOWING OR HIDING THE GRIDLINES

You can hide the border of the tables which is displayed by default (single, continuous black border with a line thickness of ½ point).

To do this, proceed as follows:

1. Open the Table menu.

2. Click on the Hide Gridlines option.

In Web pages, the default setting for tables is without a border.

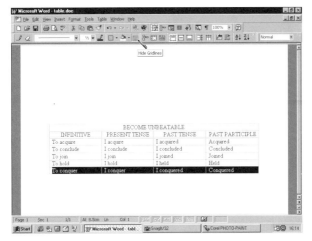

Figure 8.19: The Show/Hide Gridlines icon

The Show/Hide Gridlines icon of the Table menu shows or hides the dotted gridlines. The gridlines show the outline of the cell in which you are working but do not appear when the document is printed.

USING AUTOFORMAT

To use AutoFormat, proceed as follows:

1. Select the table.

2. Open the Table menu.

3. Click on the Table AutoFormat option.

4. Select, for example, Contemporary from the 40 available formats.

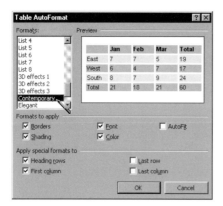

Figure 8.20: The Contemporary format from the Table AutoFormat menu

CONVERTING A TABLE TO TEXT AND VICE-VERSA

For various reasons, a table may be converted to text. In this case, the columns are replaced by tabs, commas, paragraph marks and other separators. It is also possible to reverse the process, provided that tabs have been inserted between what will become columns.

1. Select the rows or the entire table that you want to convert to text.

2. Open the Table menu.

3. Click on the Convert Table to Text option.

4. Select the separators you wish to use.

ADDING NUMBERS IN A ROW OR COLUMN

To add numbers inside your table:

1. Click on the cell in which the total is to appear.

2. Open the Table menu.

3. Choose the Formula option.

• If the cell you have selected is at the bottom of a column of numbers, Word proposes the formula =SUM(ABOVE).

• If the cell you have selected is on the right-hand side of a row of numbers, Word proposes the formula =SUM(LEFT).

4. Click on OK to confirm.

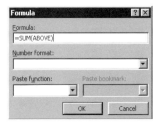

Figure 8.21: Perform calculations in Word 97

Word incorporates effective calculation functions. The standard settings are either A2:C4 type references or references to bookmarks or the predefined values, such as above, left and right.

Hour 9

The Outline view

THE CONTENTS FOR THIS HOUR

- Structuring long documents
- Creating the outline of a document
- Assigning heading levels to paragraphs
- Viewing the heading levels in outline view
- Collapsing or expanding the Outline
- Promoting or demoting by one level
- Moving paragraphs up or down
- Selecting text elements in Outline view
- Numbering an outline
- Printing an outline

In Word 97, Outline view allows you to organise long texts. It assigns to your document up to nine formatted heading levels. The advantage of this layout is that it clarifies the structure and reading of documents.

STRUCTURING LONG DOCUMENTS

Outline view is intended for structuring long documents and for offering a choice of specific formats.

Each heading level is formatted with the corresponding predefined heading style (Heading 1 to Heading 9). You can automatically assign these styles or levels to your headings. Word 97 indents each heading according to its level. These indents are only visible in Outline view.

1. Open the sample text entitled *Spreading the good word about multimedia.*

Spreading the good word about multimedia

CD-ROM editors are faced with a considerable number of obstacles.

The first problem involves combining widely-differing skills. They come from different backgrounds. They find it hard to communicate. How do you ensure that a sound engineer with no knowledge of data processing is able to work with a designer responsible for digitising sound information? They do not speak the same language. Dialogue has to be established between the artist and the technician.
The second problem is to find authors. Products may have to be located in Germany, in the United States and in other countries. Then you have to understand the target market. For example, it is no good asking $100,000 in advance for a transaction <u>and</u> expecting an assurance that you will be able to sell at least 20,000 units of the product within a year if the product is not useful to the country it is being sold in!

Figure 9.1: A document in Normal view

This document has a specific structure, composed of different levels of text, headings and sub-headings. Outline view displays this structure and allows you to make use of it.

2. Click on the Outline view icon at the extreme left of the horizontal scrolling bar located at the base of the screen just above the Status bar. You can also change to Outline view by selecting the View menu and clicking on the Outline submenu.

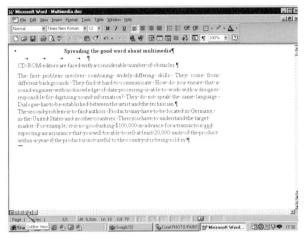

Figure 9.2: The Outline view icon at the base of the screen

The document entitled *Spreading the good word about multimedia* is displayed in Outline view.

> *It is not only possible to create an outline for an existing text, but also to begin writing a text by organising the headings.*

Familiarise yourself with each constituent element of the structure, indented according to its outline numbered level.

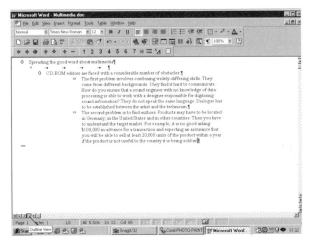

Figure 9.3: The document is displayed on the screen in Outline view

CREATING THE OUTLINE OF A DOCUMENT

There are three ways of creating an outline for a document.

- Organise a new document by typing the headings in Outline view. When you organise headings and subheadings, Word 97 automatically applies predefined heading styles to them. In order to be able to work more efficiently with your text, you can collapse it so that only the headings you are interested in are displayed. All you need to do is number the headings. To assign a level to a paragraph heading and to apply the appropriate heading style to it, drag the + or – symbols.

- Assign outline numbered levels to the paragraphs. In this way, you are applying a hierarchical structure to your document. You can work in Normal view.

- Create an Outline-type numbered list. The text is not formatted with the predefined heading styles. The Outline numbered lists extend to nine levels. You can find them by opening the Format menu and clicking on Bullets and Numbering, then clicking on the Outline Numbered tab.

Choose the second technique: assign the outline numbered levels to the paragraphs.

Work in Outline view if you need to organise and structure the content of a file.

ASSIGNING HEADING LEVELS TO PARAGRAPHS

In order to be able to work on your document in Outline view, you must assign a hierarchical structure to it. There are two ways of doing this:

- by using predefined heading styles (Heading 1 to Heading 9),

- by using heading level paragraph formats (Heading 1 to Heading 9).

If you don't want to alter the appearance of your text, use the heading levels which apply a hidden format. The heading styles modify the formatting.

Paragraph formats in Normal view

1. Work in Normal view.

2. Select the text to which you want to assign a heading level.

3. Open the Format menu.

4. Click on the Paragraph option.

5. Click on the Indents and Spacing tab.

6. Click on the required level in the Outline level box.

7. Repeat the operation as many times as there are paragraphs of different outline levels.

Your document consists of four heading levels. This is the structure assigned to your document.

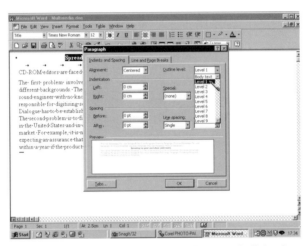

Figure 9.4: The Outline levels of the Paragraph dialog box, Indents and Spacing tab

VIEWING THE HEADING LEVELS IN OUTLINE VIEW

Once this initial work has been completed, change over to Outline view. The structure of your text appears, level by level.

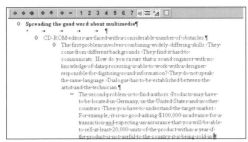

Figure 9.5: The structure assigned to your document

The Outline view allows you, with the aid of the icons numbered from 1 to 7, to view the heading levels of your text.

Figure 9.6: Viewing Level 1 headings

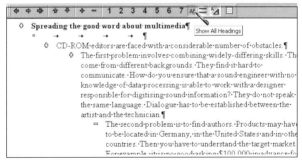

Figure 9.7: Your entire document is displayed

- If you click on the icon showing two parallel black lines, you will see the structure of your text, together with the first line of each paragraph.

- If you click on the A/A icon, you will see the format of your document.

COLLAPSING OR EXPANDING THE OUTLINE

- Collapsing an outline means that only the higher levels are displayed at the starting point.

- Expanding an outline up to a certain level means that all the headings below this level are displayed.

To collapse or expand an outline, use the numbered icons on the Outline view Toolbar.

The principle is as follows: click on the number which corresponds to the number of heading levels you want to display. To display all the levels, all you have to do is click on the All icon in the Outline view Toolbar.

If you click on the 4 and then on the icon showing a minus sign, you will obtain Level 3.

$4 - 1 = 3$

If you click on the 2 and then on the icon showing a plus sign, you will obtain Level 3.

$2 + 1 = 3$

To collapse or expand the heading levels, you can also use the Collapse and Expand icons on the Outline view Toolbar or the + and – marks of the outline.

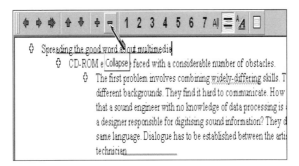

Figure 9.8: Collapsing the heading levels

PROMOTING OR DEMOTING BY ONE LEVEL

Promoting or demoting headings (moving them up or down) means that they are raised or lowered by one level.

To do this, you have two tools at your disposal: the right green arrow and the left green arrow.

- The left green arrow on the Outline view Toolbar promotes the selected paragraph to the level of the next highest heading.

- The right green arrow on the Outline view Toolbar demotes the selected paragraph to the level of the next lowest heading.

If you want to work on the structure of your document, move a heading from one level to the other, then use the green arrows indicating left and right.

Our example – *The CD-ROM market* – has the same outline numbered level as *CD-ROM editors are faced with a considerable number of obstacles*. If you feel that this is an error and that this heading should appear on the same level as the main title *Spreading the good word about multimedia*:

1. Select *The CD-ROM market*.

2. Click on the green arrow pointing to the left. Your heading is promoted by one level and is positioned on the same level as *Spreading the good word about multimedia*.

This is a very useful exercise if you have a text consisting of several hundred pages. While working in Outline view, you can modify the structure of your text as you please. The list of contents is generated as the text is entered.

MOVING PARAGRAPHS UP OR DOWN

You can use the green arrows, one pointing downward and one pointing upward, to move paragraphs.

- The green upward-pointing arrow not only moves the selected paragraph upward but also the collapsed (and temporarily hidden) text adjacent to it. It places everything above the displayed paragraph which precedes it.

- The green downward-pointing arrow not only moves the selected paragraph downward but also the collapsed (and temporarily hidden) text adjacent to it. It places everything below the displayed paragraph which follows it.

SELECTING TEXT ELEMENTS IN OUTLINE VIEW

In Outline view, the way text, headings or paragraphs are selected is different from the method used in Normal view.

To select a heading, its subheadings and the body text:

1. Click on the recessed white cross near the heading or place the pointer to the left of the heading.

2. Double-click when the pointer changes into a white arrow pointing to the right.

To select only a heading without its subheadings and paragraphs:

1. Place the pointer to the left of the heading.

2. Click when the pointer changes into a white arrow pointing to the right.

To select a paragraph of body text:

1. Either click on the little empty white square next to the paragraph or place the pointer to the left of the paragraph.

2. Click when the pointer changes into a white arrow pointing to the right.

To select a number of headings or paragraphs:

1. Place the pointer to the left of the text.

2. Move the pointer up or down according to the text elements to be selected when the pointer changes into a recessed white arrow pointing to the right.

 In Outline view, if you click once to the left of a paragraph, the entire paragraph is selected.

NUMBERING AN OUTLINE

Once your text has been structured and turned into an outline you can then number it.

To do this, perform the following operations in sequence.

1. Open the Format menu.

2. Click on the Bullets and Numbering option.

3. Select the type of outline numbering you require.

You can customise the outline at any time by clicking on the Customize option.

The settings available for customising your numbered list include:

- Numbering format

- Numbering style

- Position of the numbers

- Indent in relation to the text

- Alignment of the numbers

- The style to be applied

- And the options, such as Legal Numbering.

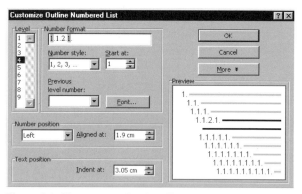

Figure 9.9: Your customised outline numbered list

To number your outline, click on each heading level, then confirm.

Figure 9.10: The numbering applied to the first part of your outline

PRINTING AN OUTLINE

Once your document has been structured in different outline levels, you can decide whether just to print the outline text or certain hierarchical levels of the text.

In Outline view:

1. Display, for example, Level 1.

2. Click on Print.

Word 97 prints only the displayed hierarchical levels. If the body text is visible, it will be printed in its entirety.

Hour 10

Mail Merge

THE CONTENTS FOR THIS HOUR

- Creating a database
- Creating a form letter
- Viewing the result of a Mail Merge
- Printing a form letter
- Printing the mailing
- Adjusting the Merge settings
- Filtering the records
- Sorting the records
- Creating mailing labels
- Printing labels while merging an address list

CREATING A DATABASE

Mail Merge, otherwise known as mailing, involves the creation of personalised documents from a database and a form letter. The form letter is a normal Word document.

The principle of the merging process is to combine the form letter and the elements of the database.

Let us say you are the Principal of a college. To assist with your correspondence with parents, you are going to create a form letter and a 'Parents' file in your database. This method can also be applied to a 'Client' file, which can be used for commercial correspondence for example.

▬▬▬ Choosing a form letter

1. Open the File menu.

2. Select the New option.

3. Click on the Letters and Faxes tab.

4. Choose your form letter.

Figure 10.1: A template for a professional letter

Opening Mail Merge

The second stage is to utilise the Mail Merge function.

1. Open the Tools menu.

2. Click on Mail Merge.

The Mail Merge Helper dialog box appears on the screen.

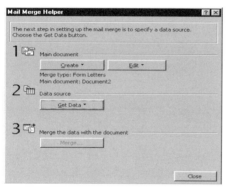

Figure 10.2: The Mail Merge Helper dialog box

3. Click on Create.

4. Choose the Form Letters option.

5. Choose the Active Window.

6. Click on the Get Data button.

7. Click on the Create Data Source button.

Word 97 offers you a list of commonly used field names. You can delete or add any names of your choice.

For a mailing addressed to the parents of students, the Name, Address, City and PostalCode fields are sufficient.

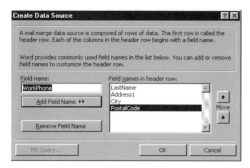

Figure 10.3: Select the appropriate fields

8. Confirm by clicking on OK.

9. Assign a name to your file.

10. Call this new file Parents.

11. Record this new file in the H10 folder for the tenth hour of this course.

12. In the fields, enter the name and address of the first two parents:

    Baker
    18 Fern Road
    Norwich
    NR1 3JC

Add this first completed file to your database, the Parents file, by clicking on Add.

Repeat the operation for the other 5 Parents files:

    Butler
    32 Nettle Road
    Norwich
    NR3 5AC

Davidson
28 Tulip Road
Norwich
NR14 8SC

Finch
45 Rose Road
Norwich
NR6 7QL

Lawrence
11 Begonia Road
Norwich
NR2 4LG

White
81 Laurel Road
Norwich
NR11 2AD

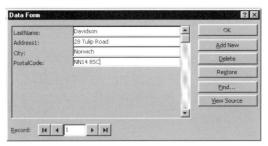

Figure 10.4: Enter the data

You can delete and add files, modify them and search for them.
When the work has been completed, confirm by clicking on OK.

From now on, only the form letter will appear on the screen.

1. Place the insertion point at the position in the letter where the Name merge field is to appear.

2. Open the Insert Merge Field box on the Mail Merge Toolbar.

Figure 10.5: Use the Insert Merge Field icon on the Mail Merge Toolbar

3. Click on the first Name field that appears.

4. Confirm.

The word 'Name' appears on your form letter.

5. Repeat this operation for the other three fields: Address, City and PostalCode.

Figure 10.6: Your form letter with the fields inserted

CREATING A FORM LETTER

Once the fields have been inserted, type your letter, consisting of:

• the name of the establishment:

The John Innes College

- its address:

  22 – 26 Castle Street Norwich, NR2 5HE

- the date:

  20 October, 1998

- the subject:

  Report and discussion periods

- the text:

  Dear Parents,
  I have pleasure in enclosing the Report on your son.
  For the next two months, we will be holding discussion periods
  every Thursday from 4.30 p.m. to 5.30 p.m.
  We will be at your disposal to answer any questions you may
  have regarding the next course of studies for your son.
  Yours sincerely,

- the signature:

  Alexander Raynor, Principal

VIEWING THE RESULT OF A MAIL MERGE

Click on the Merge to a New Document icon to view the result of
your merge operation.

The merge has taken place. Word 97 has merged your form letter
with the Parents File database. Your letter and the inserted fields
are immediately forwarded to another document which has the name
Form Letters1.

*The Merge Errors icon indicates errors which are
preventing merging in the main document or the data
source. You can correct the errors before proceeding with
the merge.*

¶
The·John·Innes·College¶
27-–-26·Castle·Street¶
Norwich¶
NR2·5HE¶
¶
20th·October·1998¶

·¶
Mr·&·Mrs·Baker¶
18·Fern·Road¶
Norwich¶
NR1·3JC¶

Figure 10.7: Merging the Mr and Mrs Baker address to the Form Letters1 document

PRINTING A FORM LETTER

To print your form letter, from the Form Letters1 document simply click on the Print icon. A single letter will be printed, the one addressed to Mr and Mrs Baker.

PRINTING THE MAILING

To print your entire mailshot, addressed to six sets of parents of students:

1. Select your merge document.

2. Click on the Merge to Printer icon.

This function performs the merge then prints the result.

Your six letters are printed.

ADJUSTING THE MERGE SETTINGS

If you want to apply changes to the printout of this mailing, open the Mail Merge dialog box.

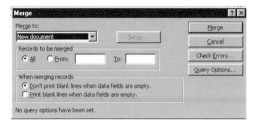

Figure 10.8: The Mail Merge dialog box in which you can define the current merge options

For example, you can request:

- selection of the records, for example those running from File Three to File Six. To do this, click on the section entitled Records to be Merged.

- a merge to a fax. To do this, open the section entitled Merge to: and select Fax.

FILTERING THE RECORDS

If you do not want to merge all the information of the data file, you can specify merge conditions.

Query Options allows you to select data records from a data source. To access these Query Options, proceed as follows:

1. Click on the Mail Merge icon on the Mail Merge toolbar.

2. Click on the Query Options button.

You then have a choice of two tabs: Filter Records and Sort Records. Filter Records means record selection.

Let us assume that you do not want to record any names in your file which begin with the letters A to D:

3. Click on the Filter Records tab.

4. Click on the Name data field in the Field panel.

5. Click on the Greater than or equal comparison formula in the Comparison: panel.

6. Enter the criterion D in the Compare to: panel.

To specify more than one comparison criterion, click on And, or on Or, in order to link them to each other.

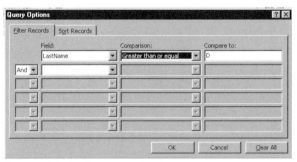

Figure 10.9: Define your selection criterion

SORTING THE RECORDS

To merge the records into a specific sequence, click on the Sort Records tab, then on the fields which are to act as selection criteria. For example, you can decide to print your Parents file in descending alphabetical order.

1. Select the Name field in the Sort by text panel.

2. Click on the Descending option.

Figure 10.10: Select the Name field to sort your files into alphabetical order

CREATING MAILING LABELS

Mailing labels are produced in the same way, with the additional option of being able to define the size of the label.

1. Open the Tools menu.

2. Click on Mail Merge.

3. Open the Create submenu.

4. Select the Mailing Labels option.

In the Product Number panel, select a type of label which is the same size as yours – the Avery standard, L2160 Mini Address.

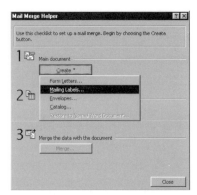

Figure 10.11: Create mailing labels

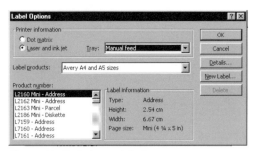

Figure 10.12: Select a label type

To learn more, click on the Details button to display information about:

- the size of the address

- the size of the top margin

- the size of the side margin

- the height of the label

- the width of the label

- the size of the paper

180

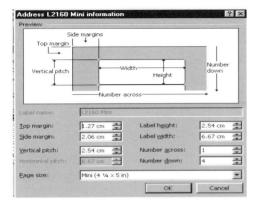

Figure 10.13: The format of the selected label

If the format and layout of the labels do not correspond to those of the labels you have created, click on Cancel.

If the format and layout of the labels do correspond to those of the labels you have created, use the selected label.

Label reference

In the Label Options dialog box:

1. Check the type of printer.

2. Click on New Label.

3. Enter a label name in the Label Reference panel.

4. Click on OK to confirm.

The new label is displayed in the Product Number panel in the form Personalised Label Name. Your Avery® label is displayed in the Product Number panel in the form Personalised Label Name.

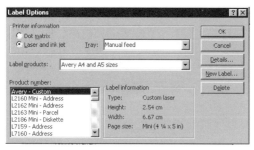

Figure 10.14: Avery is displayed in the Product Number panel

Take precise measurements of your labels. The dimensions indicated on the packet may be slightly smaller or larger than the actual sizes. Although they may differ in size by only a few millimetres, this can have a decisive effect on printing.

PRINTING LABELS WHILE MERGING AN ADDRESS LIST

The Address Book

1. Open the Tools menu.

2. Select the Mail Merge option.

3. Click on the Active Window button. The active document becomes your main merge document.

4. Click on Get Data.

5. Select the Open Data Source option.

6. Open your address book.

Your address book appears in the Header Record Delimiters section of the Mail Merge Helper dialog box.

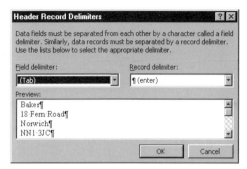

Figure 10.15: Your address book is merged

Once the data source has been defined, define the data source for your address book, then display the Word message:

7. Click on the Prepare option.

8. Select the type of printer and the type of label.

9. Insert the merge fields from your address book into the Labels dialog box.

10. Click on Merge in the Mail Merge Helper dialog box.

11. In the Merge to... dialog box, click on Printer.

Figure 10.16: Insert the merge fields of the address book

Creating an address list

You have just printed mailing labels by merging a list of existing addresses in your personal address book.

The procedure is slightly different if you have to create the address list:

1. Open the Tools menu.

2. Select the Mail Merge option.

3. Click on the Active Window button. The active document becomes your main merge document.

4. Click on Get Data.

5. Click on Create Data Source.

6. Define the records. Each of the data sources constitutes a record.

The first line, known as the header line, contains the names of the merge fields. Word 97 displays a list of commonly used field names.

7. Delete or add the names of your choice.

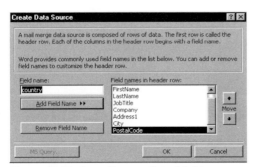

Figure 10.17: Compile your list of fields

Hour 11

Printing

THE CONTENTS FOR THIS HOUR

- Learning about the Print dialog box
- Using the Control Panel
- Installing a printer
- Selecting the text to be printed
- Specifying the number of copies
- Printing even and odd pages
- Choosing the print options
- Printing the properties of a document
- Using different types of paper in the same document
- Selecting a paper tray
- Cancelling a print job

LEARNING ABOUT THE PRINT DIALOG BOX

A printer which has been installed in Windows is automatically accessible in Word 97. Printing is therefore a very straightforward operation.

The first step is to open the File menu, then to click on the Print option and view the Print dialog box which appears on the screen.

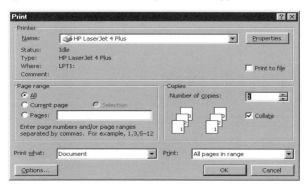

Figure 11.1: The Print dialog box

A list of different options is displayed on the screen. The first, and most obvious, is the choice of printer. If you click on the Name option, you will see a list of the printers installed on your PC. If you are using only one printer, it will be permanently selected. If the name of your printer does not appear in the list, this means that it has not been installed.

USING THE CONTROL PANEL

The system makes reference only to the installed printer. Let us consider the case where management has provided an employee with a colour printer. The employee uses this printer in only 10% of cases, when printing reports which include diagrams in colour. Despite this, the colour printer was entered in the list of available printers. To do this, the employee opened the Print File in the Control Panel and then, with the aid of a floppy disk or CD-ROM, installed the driver for the peripheral device in question. From then on, the system was aware that two printers were installed. In Windows, the existence of additional printers indicates only the presence of the peripheral driver. This does not signify that the printer in question is switched on, or even that it has already been connected to the PC via a cable. To change from one printer to another, it is necessary only to click on the appropriate list. To change printers you must open the Control Panel. The procedure is as follows:

1. Click on the Start button on the Taskbar.

2. Select the Settings submenu.

3. Choose Control Panel.

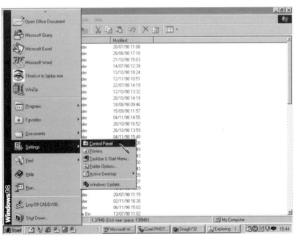

Figure 11.2: Access the Control Panel

INSTALLING A PRINTER

The Control Panel is displayed on the screen.

Figure 11.3: The Printers option in the Control Panel

4. Click on the Printers icon.

You are offered two choices.

- Add Printer.
- Icons for the printers already installed on your system. In our system, this is the HP Laserjet 4.

The Add Printer Wizard

Figure 11.4: Select one of the two options

5. Select the Add Printer option. The Add Printer Wizard helps you to install your printer without delay.

6. Click on the Have Disk button if the new printer to be installed has been supplied with an installation floppy disk. A dialog box prompts you to insert the floppy disk containing the printer driver. The default drive is A.

7. In the list of available ports, select the printer port you wish to use.

8. Click on Next.

9. If necessary, configure the printer port by clicking on the Configure Port button.

10. In the dialog box, assign a name to your printer (you can also retain the name assigned by the printer manufacturer).

11. If you want this printer to be the default printer, select the Yes option. If not, choose No.

12. Click on Finish. Word prompts you to insert the Word 97 installation disk.

13. Insert the installation disk containing the new printer driver.

14. Confirm by clicking on OK.

15. Enter the access path for your new printer driver.

As soon as the operation has been completed, Word 97 displays the Printer dialog box again.

1. Open the File menu.

2. Choose Print.

3. Click on the Properties command button.

4. In the Properties dialog box of the selected printer, click on the Paper tab and configure the most relevant options.

For example:

- The paper size.

- Tray A.

- Orientation of the paper: landscape (i.e. horizontal) or portrait (i.e. vertical).

- The printer memory.

- Grayscale.

Figure 11.5: The Add Printer Wizard helps you to install your printer

Printer already installed

If you click on the Printer already installed option, namely the HP Laserjet 4, you can see details of the document currently being printed:

- Name of the document.

- Status.

- Property.

- Number of bytes already printed.

- The starting date and time of the current print job.

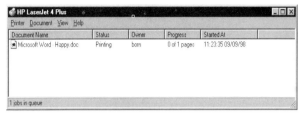

Figure 11.6: Details of the current print job

SELECTING THE TEXT TO BE PRINTED

You have now installed your choice of printer. You now want to select the documents to be printed.

Proceed as follows.

1. Open the File menu.

2. Select Print. The Printer text panel is now updated to correspond with your entries in the Control Panel.

3. Choose one of the three options displayed in the Page range panel:

- All: if you select All, your entire document will be printed.

- Current page: if you choose this option, only the page containing the insertion point will be printed.

- Pages: if you select this option, you must specify which pages you want to print. If you want to print page 2, enter 2. Let us say your document runs to 7 pages and you want to print pages 4 to 6, you must enter 4-6 in the number panel. Remember to enter the hyphen between the two numbers.

SPECIFYING THE NUMBER OF COPIES

To specify the number of copies:

1. Open the File menu.

2. Select Print.

3. In the number panel, indicate the number of copies you require. Let us assume your document covers two pages:

- If the Collate box is ticked, Word 97 first prints the complete set, page 1 and page 2, then prints the duplicate copies.

- If the Collate box is not ticked, Word 97 first prints two copies of page 1, then two copies of page 2.

PRINTING EVEN AND ODD PAGES

1. In the File menu, choose Print.

2. When the dialog box appears, choose the appropriate option in the Print panel.

CHOOSING THE PRINT OPTIONS

To choose the print options, proceed as follows.

1. In the File menu, choose Print.

2. Click on the Options button in the Print dialog box.

3. In the dialog box which appears, click on the Print tab and tick the boxes corresponding to the options you require.

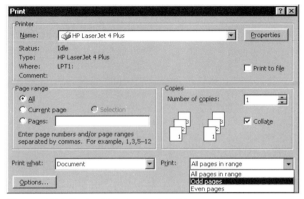

Figure 11.7: Under Print, select Odd pages

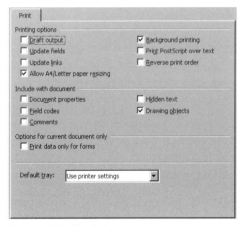

Figure 11.8: The Print tab

In the Print tab, you are offered three sets of options:

- Printing options
- Include with document
- Default tray

The print options are:

- **Draft output**: in draft output, Word 97 does not print the layout and omits the majority of the graphics.

- **Update fields**: this checks the status of the files in the database to see whether or not they have been updated.

- **Update links**: the print job takes account of the latest modifications made to a linked object, a drawing for example (.bmp format) linked to a text file (.doc format).

- **Allow A4/Letter paper resizing**: check this box if you want Word to automatically adjust documents formatted for another country's standard paper size.

- **Background printing**: you can continue to work while your document is being printed, provided that the RAM memory and the hard disk of your PC are large enough to allow your other work to proceed at the normal speed. Background printing uses more system memory. To speed up the printing process, deactivate this check box.

- **Print PostScript over text**: you can send PostScript programming strings to your printer by inserting Print fields in the text of the document. Word 97 transmits commands to the printer in the form of native PostScript codes. The PostScript codes incorporated in your document are executed according to their sequence of insertion. This only concerns a few users.

- **Reverse print order**: Word 97 prints the documents beginning with the last page.

PRINTING THE PROPERTIES OF A DOCUMENT

You can print the properties of a document, together with information such as comments, hidden text or drawings.

▬▬ Printing the properties without printing the document

It is possible to print the properties of the document without printing the document itself:

1. Open the File menu.

2. Choose Print. The Print dialog box is displayed.

3. Click on Document properties in the Print what: panel.

▬▬ Printing the properties and the document

You can also print your document at the same time as its properties or comments, annotations, markers, field codes, hidden text, drawings, etc.

1. Open the Tools menu.

2. Click on Options.

3. Select the Print tab.

4. In the section Include with document, tick the boxes which correspond to the special characters you want to appear in your document during printing.

You can print AutoText entries. Open the File menu, click on Print and, in the Print what: panel, select AutoText entries.

USING DIFFERENT TYPES OF PAPERS IN THE SAME DOCUMENT

Not all printers support this function.

1. Open the File menu.

2. Select Page Setup.

3. Click on the Paper Source tab.

- To specify the paper tray required for your first document page, click on the required paper source in the First page panel.

- To specify a paper tray for printing the subsequent pages, click on the required paper tray in the Other pages panel.

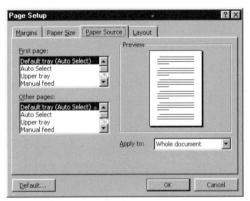

Figure 11.9: Select the two paper trays

If it is part of a document and not just one page, in the Apply to: panel, choose Selected sections, then click on the section concerned before specifying the paper tray.

Selecting a paper tray

To select a paper tray:

1. Open the File menu.

2. Choose Print.

3. Click on the Properties button. The paper tray can be:

- The default tray (upper tray)

- The lower tray

- Manual feed

- Manual envelope feed

Cancelling a print job

There are three ways of cancelling a print job:

- Click on Cancel.

- Press ESC if background printing is deactivated.

- Double-click on the Print icon in the Status bar.

If you print a small document and background printing is activated, the Printer icon may not appear long enough in the Status bar to enable you to click on it.

Hour 12

Surfing the Internet

THE CONTENTS FOR THIS HOUR

- Linking up with the Internet
- Selecting the Web Toolbar
- Opening and customising the Welcome Page
- Searching the Web
- Opening Favorites
- The Go button
- Adding an FTP site to the list of Internet sites
- Creating Hypertext links
- Stopping the search for a link

The Internet for commerce

In the past, companies had to rent special lines in order to relay data from one branch office to another. They used to despatch couriers and they called in accountants and analysts. Nowadays, with the benefits of the Internet and encrypted data (data to which a secret code is assigned in order to maintain confidentiality), similar information is exchanged virtually instantaneously by the simple expedient of a local telephone call.

The Internet for the Arts

For the artist and writer, working via the Internet is an opportunity to get in touch with friends, editors, magazines and journals without spending money on postage. Emulation, research and production are realised via the network of networks.

The Internet for those who want to know more

The Internet places an entire planet at the disposal of the user. Those connected to it finally have the possibility of not only gaining instant access to a vast amount of information, they are also able to act upon it. There is interaction between those who generate and those who consume the information. Dialogue is now possible.

LINKING UP WITH THE INTERNET

To gain access to the Internet, you must have a modem and an Internet account with an Internet service provider (ISP); alternatively, you can, if appropriate, simply use the network at your place of work.

If you have these facilities but you have so far been unable to get onto the Internet, it may simply be that the site you want to visit is too busy. Be patient. Try again later.

SELECTING THE WEB TOOLBAR

The Web Toolbar gives you rapid access to documents containing hyperlinks. You can use this toolbar to open the Start Page or the Welcome Page on the Internet.

The Web Toolbar allows you to add to the Favorites file any documents of particular interest you find on the Internet. The Web Toolbar keeps a record of the last 10 documents you have accessed with the aid of this same toolbar or by using a hyperlink.

To find the Web Toolbar:

1. Open the View menu.

2. Click on Toolbars.

3. Select Customize.

4. Tick the Web check box.

The Web Toolbar is displayed on the screen.

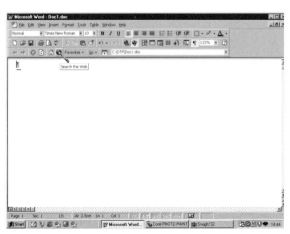

Figure 12.1: The Web Toolbar

Word 97

In Word 97, the Web Toolbar allows you to access your Web documents (html, Jpeg, Gif and animated Gif format) on the hard disk (working offline) as well as on the network once connection has been established.

OPENING AND CUSTOMISING THE WELCOME PAGE

The Start Page is the first page to be displayed in the navigator when you start the Web Navigator. The Start Page can be any Web site or a document on the hard disk of your PC. You can open this Start Page from the Web Toolbar. A Start Page may contain hypertext links to other documents on your PC.

Before choosing a Start Page, you must start Netscape Navigator.

1. Open the View menu.
2. Click on the Toolbars option.
3. Click on Web.
4. Select Welcome Page.

Customising the Web Start Page

1. Open the document you want to use as the Start Page.
2. Click on the Go menu on the Web Toolbar.
3. Click on Set Start Page.
4. Click on Yes.

The Start Page icon initiates the default Internet connection program which you have installed on Internet Explorer or on Netscape, according to your preference. In the context of this example, and without prejudice, we have chosen Netscape.

Figure 12.2: Customising the Web Start Page

To access the Navigator, click on its icon. You may be surprised to find that the Welcome Page is different from the one indicated in the user preferences; instead it is the Microsoft Network Welcome Page. This means that Microsoft is displaying its own site by default.

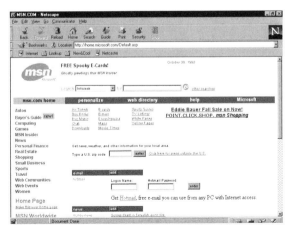

Figure 12.3: Microsoft displays its own site by default

The Welcome Page is normally used to initiate navigation. The most logical approach is to utilise the Alta Vista or Yahoo! search engines for example. In certain cases, when used for the first time, MSN prompts you to download a supplementary program (plug-in), such as Future Splash. Microsoft is making its contribution to the Internet by developing products intended to improve the interface. If this Welcome Page takes a long time to load, two control elements are provided. The first step is to look in the Status Bar at the base of the screen. Details of the current display are shown as a percentage. If the downloading times are excessive, simply deselect the image loading option. This increases the speed by a factor of 7 to 8. If you are using Netscape, avoid purely Microsoft-generated plug-ins. They are obviously intended to exclude non-Microsoft products. The reason for this is that Microsoft is hoping to distance itself from the competition by supplying proprietary Netscape improvements.

SEARCHING THE WEB

To search for addresses on the Web:

1. Click on the Search the Web icon on the Web Toolbar.

This tool allows access to the Microsoft Search Page. It selects a search engine from the main search engines available.

2. In the text panel of the search engine, enter the name of the site you wish to visit. Let us suppose that a Scotsperson on the other side of the world wishes to access the *Scotsman* newspaper but has forgotten the Internet address.

As soon as the search has been confirmed, by clicking on the Search button, the system is activated.

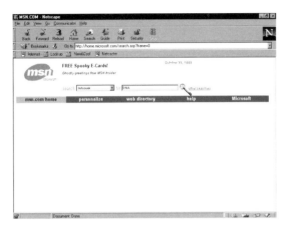

Figure 12.4: Use a search engine to locate your site

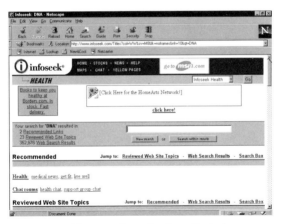

Figure 12.5: The search engine is activated

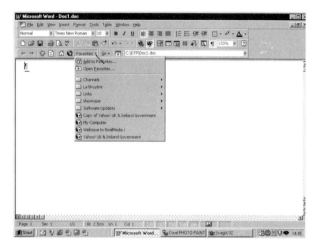

Figure 12.6: The Welcome Page of the located site is displayed on the screen

After a certain period has elapsed, the responses from the search engine are displayed on the screen.

OPENING FAVORITES

The Favorites button allows rapid access to the sites marked with a bookmark. When you open a document on the World Wide Web, or on the hard disk, add it to the Favorites file. This will allow you to open it next time without the need to enter its path name.

To perform this operation:

1. In the View menu, click on Toolbars.

2. Click on Web. The Web Toolbar is displayed.

3. Open the Favorites menu on the Web Toolbar.

4. Select the Add to Favorites submenu.

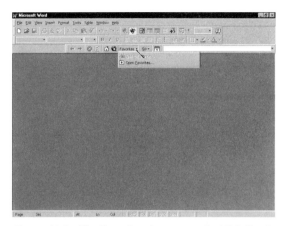

Figure 12.7: The Favorites button on the Web Toolbar

THE GO BUTTON

This tool provides a shortcut in order to access those addresses you have previously visited. This acts as a chronological history of the visits.

There are four other tools situated at the left-hand edge of the bar:

- Stop the Link Search: Stop the Site Search: if the search period is very long, the user may exit and stop.

- Refresh the Active Page: in the event of a poorly-executed display, with loss of data, the display can be corrected by refreshing it.

- Previous: this accesses the previous file visited.

- Next: this accesses the next document in the History.

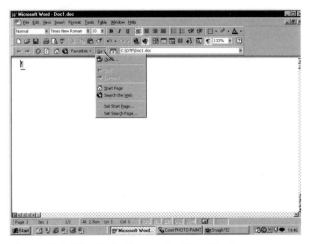

Figure 12.8: The Go button on the Web Toolbar

Recently used files

The History contains the list of web page names and the files you have already viewed by following the hypertext links in the Office programs and on the Internet. To open a file which has been recently logged in Word, all you have to do is click on the first filename that appears at the bottom of the File menu.

You can program this list yourself and decide whether or not it should be displayed.

To do this, proceed as follows:

1. Open the Tools menu.

2. Choose Options.

3. Click on the General tab.

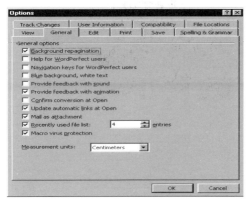

Figure 12.9: Displaying the Recently used files list

4. Activate the Recently used files list check box if you want to view the recently used files at the bottom of the File menu. You can view up to a maximum of nine files.

5. Deactivate the Recently used files list check box if you do not want to view the History of your most recent visits at the bottom of the File menu.

ADDING AN FTP SITE TO THE LIST OF INTERNET SITES

You can add an FTP (File Transfer Protocol) site to the list of Internet sites.

To do this, proceed as follows:

1. Open the File menu.

2. Click on Open.

3. In the Look in: panel, click on Add/Modify FTP Locations.

4. Enter the name of the FTP site you wish to visit, for example, in the Name of the FTP site panel in the Add/Modify FTP Locations dialog box.

5. If you want to connect to an FTP site which permits anonymous connections, click on Anonymous in the Begin Session panel in the Add/Modify FTP Locations dialog box.

6. If you want to connect to an FTP site which is reserved for users with a password, click on the User option in the Begin Session panel in the add/Modify FTP Locations dialogue box.

Figure 12.10: Adding an FTP address

Figure 12.11: You can make an anonymous connection to an FTP site

CREATING HYPERTEXT LINKS

You can embellish your Web pages and your Word publications by inserting hypertext links, also referred to as hyperlinks. The hypertext link is a point of contact which allows you to move from one location to another. This location may be a file on your hard disk, an Internet address, a bookmark or multimedia files containing videos and sound.

The field of your hypertext link includes text which appears highlighted in blue. All you need to do is to click on the text in order to move immediately to the required location.

You can insert your own hypertext links.

1. Open the Insert menu.

2. Click on the Hypertext Link command. The Insert a Hypertext Link dialog box appears on the screen.

Insert Hyperlink

Link to file or URL:

http://www.tavelocity.com | Browse...

Enter or locate the path to the document you want to link to. This can be an Internet address (URL), a document on your hard drive, or a document on your company's network.

Path: http://www.tavelocity.com/

Named location in file (optional):

| Browse...

If you want to jump to a specific location within the document, such as a bookmark, a named range, a database object, or a slide number, enter or locate that information above.

☑ Use relative path for hyperlink

OK | Cancel

Figure 12.12: Insert your Hypertext link

3. Enter the path of the document to which you want to insert a link.

4. Alternatively, search for and then enter the path of the document to which you want to insert a link.

5. If you want to locate a specific point in the document, such as a bookmark or a named page, enter this information in the Location in the File panel. This is an optional function.

STOPPING THE SEARCH FOR A LINK

To cancel a time-consuming transfer (the search times may extend to several minutes), you must display the Web Toolbar.

1. Open the View menu.

2. Click on Toolbars.

3. Activate Web.

4. Click on the Stop Link icon as soon as the Web Toolbar appears.

The Stop Search for a Link button is accessible only if you open or activate a file on the Internet, on the World Wide Web or on your company's Intranet (a local network); it is not accessible if the file is located on your hard disk or on the network.

Index

Word 97

M

 N

O

 P

R

Replacing
a word 88

S

Saving
a document 47
Screen
Word 97 16
Screen Tips 20
Scroll bars 37
Searching
for information on the
Web 204
Selecting
cells 138
fonts 60
Settings
3D WordArt 120
Size
character 8
Shading
a border 56
Spelling
correcting 43
Starting
programs 7
Statistics 96
Styles 79
automatic 79
changing 76

creating 74
printing 79
Synonyms 92

T

Tables
adding borders to 149
creating 136
equalising columns and
rows 146
inserting columns 142
inserting rows 141
Templates
creating 82
Text
adding styles to 61
columns 104
cutting 56
fitting around irregular
objects 131
Time 68
Title bar 18
Toolbars
customising 19
Format 9
Web 201
Tools
menu 10

U

Undo, move 42

V

W

ALT

ù 0249   à 0224   è 0232

é 0233   ê 0234   É 0201

á 0225   Ê 0202   â 0226

ç 0231